JOURNEY
OF THE
STAR CHILDREN THROUGH TIME

A True Love Story for the Ages Covering
Nearly Seventy Years and Two Continents

Sonja Christiansen, KRMT/Ed Webber,RMT

BALBOA.PRESS
A DIVISION OF HAY HOUSE

Balboa Press books may be ordered through booksellers or by contacting:

Balboa Press
A Division of Hay House
1663 Liberty Drive
Bloomington, IN 47403
www.balboapress.com
844-682-1282

Print information available on the last page.

ISBN: 978-1-9822-7877-9 (sc)
ISBN: 978-1-9822-7879-3 (hc)
ISBN: 978-1-9822-7878-6 (e)

Library of Congress Control Number: 2022900403

Balboa Press rev. date: 01/10/2022

This is the guide you have been looking for
to help you through the spiritual world of energies,
out-of-body flights, walking on fire,
prophetic dreams, and so much more.

Bring your light.

Contents

Acknowledgments

A heartfelt thank you to everyone near and far who
participated both early and late in this endeavor, supporting
our efforts over the years in so many different ways to
create this true book of breathtaking adventures.

Jackie and Sue Martin
(my sisters from another mother)
Elizabeth Hoy
Arla Calleach Collett, "Keeper of The Earth"
Juni Moon
Jena and Mark McDonald
Kelly Sarro
Nathan Harper, MS, APRN-CNP,
Gay Dyson
Alija Huseinbasic
Jill Stinson
Autumn Cole
Erica Ruby Christiansen
Rhonda Hunt McCarthy,
Karen and Eddy Owens
A. R. Buchanan of Good Words Ink
for editing and organizing work
James Nelson of Meditation Warriors
for his insight, guidance, help with electronics, attention
to detail, and graceful dealing with midnight calls

A special thank-you to all of our extended family who have
supported us through our frustrations as well as our joy. So
many have put their time and life energy into supporting,
listening, and discussing our ideas and teachings and offering

their truthful feelings about our beliefs and understandings. Thank you for helping us negotiate through the weft and warp of our bits and pieces of chatter and the rearrangement of words over the years as soon as new words appeared and needed to be coaxed into place. It's been nearly twenty years of listening, correcting, rewording, giving up, and starting again. We could not have completed this without the positive energy and support from all of you, as well as many more who have not been listed. Thank you for your amazing love and support throughout the years. You have made a difference.

A special thank-you to our son Vince for his unrelenting support, even with his eyes rolling up in his head many times!

Thank you to all of our friends, family and guides over the years who have walked with us on this path. I know it seems like we have been talking about this forever! I think perhaps you are right! It's finally here! Thank you all for your patience, support, and encouragement. It has been nearly twenty years since we first laid down tracks for what this has become. We could not have continued without your love and encouragement. We hope you are happy with the outcome and that we have been able to bring light. Without your loving and sometimes tough guidance, we would never have been able to get here.

With Love,
S. and The Fuzzy Guy

We hope our story will make a difference
in showing how we can all bring our
own light one spark at a time.
Thank you.

Introduction

The original intent of this book was to write our life story in tandem, sharing our learnings and understanding about Spirit and life as we figured it out and over time melded insights with many different teachers along our lives' pathway, writing our own memories and describing the paths we took in life. We hoped to offer some guidance and support for others who followed our insights and understandings as we traveled our path. We wanted to bring an understanding that those who can access their gifts and learn how to use them are light bringers, not evil or nuts.

We did start out that way but Ed, Star Eyes, passed before he could finish his work. I have gone through his notes and have tried to speak with his voice. At times you will see his name at the start of the chapter or paragraph. Those are his direct writings. I make note where I am paraphrasing his words. If there is no name on the chapter or in the story, it is a glimpse of what we shared together. We still have an amazing relationship. He is around and makes himself known. Some of his words and feelings have been channeled through me.

We hope these words, as well as our life's adventure, will touch your heart and open doors to the higher realms of awareness for you, however you believe them to be. All things are possible through love and intention. The light will guide you if you ask through your heart.

Thank you for peeking into our world. We
would love to know what you think.

Our story is offered to you with love.
Sonja and Ed (Star Shine and Star Eyes)

To our readers, just so you can keep names straight, Ed's birth name was Harvard Edgely Webber. In school he was called Harvey. When he had a son, he named him the same. As the son got older, the two of them operated a business together. So to separate the two, the son was called Harvard and the dad was called Ed. Friends of ours started calling him Fuzz because of the beard he had in later life. The name stuck with our friends and family. So you will see "Harvard," "Harvey," "Ed," and "Fuzz." All refer to the same amazing guy!

Names inside this book have been changed
to protect everyone's privacy.

Open

Somewhere in time, so long ago, two souls were finding their way through the maze of forever. They were within the depths of anonymity, searching for an identity. They found each other and compared their journeys. They came to the conclusion that together, they were one.

So it was for many turns of time, until they were brought to the council and asked to be part of a grand experiment. They were to go to a place where they would become two again. They were opposed at first, but the council explained that as two they could influence more and learn from many teachers at once. They were convinced and set forth on a wondrous journey to fulfill the wishes of the council.

In their journey, they became separated and lost, but they had memories of their purpose and did their best to learn and influence others. Then, on one turn of time, they were reunited. And as always, together they were one. And all of their training and purposes were revealed. They went on for many more turns of time, once again together in heart and purpose, to influence all those around them to the light.

—Star Eyes

Star Eyes and Star Shine

Sonja

The war was over. At least on paper. But it was not over for those who hungered, who mourned, who had lost loved ones, or who tried to make ends meet in a now upside-down economy. The year was 1946. One did what one could to get by in the German countryside. Food was rationed with ration cards. Proof of birth and "proper" family got one in line. Formerly well-heeled young women became cleaning women, "pleasure workers," babysitters, and farm laborers, as well as photographers if they were lucky enough to have cameras and connections.

So it was for a nineteen-year-old living on a farm far away from the city that had been bombed, her family gone. She found shelter with an elderly family she did not know who gave her food and lodging in trade for farm work. The young woman who had arrived at the farm with only the clothes on her back and a small Kodak camera walked into the town five miles away to sell eggs and what produce she could fit into her basket each day. How had she come by a camera? Who knows. Strange things went on in those shadowy days. She walked to town each day with her basket, along with her precious camera, guarding her secret, least she be turned out.

A cold wind blew through the November air. It was a perfect day to get house chores done and beat the rugs on the line. Suddenly water gushed out from under the oversize man's coat the young woman wore. The secret was out now, if it had not been suspected before. What could be done? The elderly family was kind. The child, who arrived well before her time, underweight and malnourished, weighed two pounds. She was wrapped quickly in

2

old bedding and placed on the back of the wood stove in a bread pan, none thinking she would live. The young mother had no milk. In winter, the cows were dry. A wet nurse was found, and food was traded. The child, having no father, was not allowed a ration card. At first milk was enough, but as the child grew, something had to be done. The young woman left the child in the care of the farm family and went into the town to earn a living—sometimes with her camera and sometimes in other ways. She would be gone for many weeks at a time.

In time, the young mother rebuilt her life and came back to get the child. The child had lived with the family as one of their own for several years. The family was not willing to give the child back now. During those years in the country, there was no paperwork, no birth certificates, no proof of purchase; children were born on the farm without benefit of doctors being present. Only the words of the family who had lived through the tumultuous times were left. They loved the child as their own.

After months of pleading and unproductive bargaining, the young mother, still standing her ground to reclaim her child, sighed and, appearing defeated, left the room.

As the glowing evening transformed into the ink of an overcast night, she crept in through the wide crack in the side of the old barn, through the summer kitchen door, and into the house proper, and then into the tiny bedroom created years prior in the back of the small kitchen fireplace. In a fast, cloaked swoop, she spirited the small child away, tenderly placing her into her large carry case, and headed for the airport with a dose or two of paregoric to make sure the child slept throughout the long flight. It was a wild ride flying through the night in a Zundapp KS side car. This world was rife with black markets where, with a bit of horse trading, one could get what one needed.

I Was Born Running

Ed

It was a chilly afternoon in early February 1947, in a small town in western Maine. The fifteen-year-old mother-to-be was in the last hours of childbirth. She was at once excited and frightened out of her wits. She had lived on a farm most of her young life with her great-grandmother and a couple of cousins. She knew what bearing young was all about but wasn't sure what she would be experiencing. She knew this one fact: she was going to have this baby, and it would be the one thing she could love and count on to love her back, for real.

Early in the morning on the 8th of February, she gave birth to a boy. She was happier in that moment than she could remember in her short life. Two days later, the man she had come to love as her father (who was actually her uncle) came to collect her and the baby from the hospital and take them home.

Home. Home? It was probably not as much a home as a house. It lasted a few months, but postwar Maine was not an easy place to make a living. So off to Staten Island, New York, she went, where her "dad" was a chauffeur and her "mother" was a cleaning woman.

My mom went to work across the river in the manufacturing plant building airplanes for the war effort, leaving me with various babysitters. Most of them wanted to adopt me, but Mom would have none of that. Eventually she and her mom moved back to Maine and lived on a houseboat for a time. One day when I was about two, my grandmother loaded Mom and me into the car and drove us to a boarding house in town and told mom to

4

get out. This was going to be her new "home." The shock was unbelievable. Here she was, seventeen with a two-year-old child and being turned out by her mother with no more than a few weeks' worth of rent and barely enough money to buy food for a few days.

Always a plucky child, Mom turned to survival mode. She took odd jobs where she could, and eventually she was able to stand on her own. I was growing like a weed and was showing some disturbing tendencies, such as a penchant for running away. One morning shortly after I turned three, she was awoken by the local police, who arrested her and took her to the station house. She told them that she had a little boy. They told her that was what they wanted to talk to her about. When she walked into the station, she saw me sitting on a matron's lap. It was then that she learned that I had gotten up early that morning and had been found naked staring up at the police officer directing traffic in the busiest intersection in town. They wanted to arrest her for child neglect. When they found out that I had piled chairs and books by the front door, climbed up, and made my escape, they thought differently. They took her home and said, "You want to watch that child; he will keep doing this!" They were right! But I had to know what was out there!

Not too long before she died, she told me that I should write my autobiography and call it "I Was Born Running and Never Stopped."

Our Mothers Helped Change the World

Our mothers may or may not have had choices about getting pregnant. But they had the ability to make different decisions about their situations. Even back in the day, there were choices. The choices may have been dangerous, but women for eons have known there are ways to terminate pregnancies. It was a hard time, and they both faced and dealt with the mores of society at the time. Birthing out of wedlock was not something that was done then. By making the choice of letting us be born, their lives changed. So did ours. Who would have thought that their children, born in different countries without fathers during wartime, would ever meet, grow up, fall in love, and work toward showing the world the connections we all have with each other? Their choices and their strength, as time unfolded, brought more light into the world and into their personal lives as well.

My First Flight

Ed

About a year after my running away incident, Mom met a man who had been severely wounded during the war. He was an amputee with what we all recently have come to know as PTSD, as well as other dysfunctions. They dated for a while, he asked her to marry him, and she accepted. They roamed around New York, Connecticut, and the New Jersey area for a few years. Dad was a machinist, and he followed several jobs for a major company around New England. During this time, he had four heart attacks, which left him unable to work at a regular job. He also had to have several surgeries on his amputation.

One night while he was chopping wood, the ax slipped and almost cut off my dad's hand. It was during that wild ride to the hospital that I had my first out-of-body experience. I was seven.

After dad was fixed up, we moved back to Maine. We lived in an old two-story farmhouse on twenty acres of woodland. It was there that I started to "fly" at will. At night, when I would go to bed, I would go to the top of the stairs and step out into a star field and soar. Some nights I would set it up to go somewhere that I had heard of. We call this remote viewing today. I would fly to India and see the great temples, or to China and see the Great Wall. I couldn't wait to go to bed to fly again.

My great-great-grandmother needed live-in care, so we moved to Cutler, Maine, and lived in her old home. She was 111 when we went there. She used to call me into her room to tell me stories about the Underground Railroad. Her home had been the last stop in that part of the country for fleeing slaves. Her husband was a ship's captain. There were secret places under the eaves of the house where slaves would hide till the tide came in, and my grandfather would then take them down to a ship and take them across the Bay of Fundy to Canada and freedom. She would also tell me stories about "Mr. Grant and Mr. Lincoln." She died at the age of 113. I still miss her.

Out-of-Body /
Remote Viewing

Ed

I believe that the reason I had this first OOB (out of body) experience was because I felt a need to escape. In my innocence, I didn't know I couldn't. I had always felt trapped. The trauma of seeing my dad with his hand dangling by a small piece of flesh with blood gushing from his wrist really shocked me, along with the fact that Mom was driving like a crazy woman. It was the first time in her life she had driven a car! I was so traumatized that I *had* to leave. So, I did. I did not go far, but just far enough so the edges were smoothed out. But now I *knew* I could do this!

They saved Dad's hand, and it worked mostly as good as new. They decided that living in a self-built log cabin in the woods in Upper Greenwood Lakes, New Jersey, wasn't what they really wanted to be doing, so back to civilization we went, ending up in Milford, Connecticut.

This placed us right on the beach. I could leave the house and jump off the sea wall and be sitting in total seclusion. No one could see me, and I could sit and draw energy from the surf as it crashed a few dozen feet in front of me, and I would sail away to places that I had only heard of in books and stories. I was free to be wherever I wanted to be, and I didn't have to stare at goats!

No one taught me or even told me about remote viewing, so I didn't have a name for it. Mom and Dad just called it an overactive imagination! I noticed they would get nervous whenever I would talk about my adventures with such clarity. Mom had never been outside of the country, but Dad had and was very familiar with the places I would describe. By that time, I hadn't acquired my huge thirst for knowledge, but that was to start very soon.

The US Army had started some experimentation with remote viewing in the late forties and early fifties, so some whispers were about in those days. It wasn't until the fifties and sixties that anybody in the public realm started talking about it. At the time, I was reading Frank Buck's *Bring 'Em Back Alive*. I was also absorbing some pretty strange stuff for a ten-year-old kid. I sure wish Wikipedia had been around then. A small-town library didn't provide much help, so when I would get to be in a larger town, I would go to their library and dig up other works that offered a broader view of life.

Simply put, remote viewing is sending your mind on a road trip while your body is relaxed in a chair or on a bed. Latter-day prophets like Tesla, Einstein, and Cacye referred to it as being in a trancelike state and being able to witness something while in that state. It was the equivalent of traveling to someplace and retaining a memory of the trip.

The government was obviously looking for a leg up on their enemies. I was simply looking for ways to escape. Things at home were getting worse every year. I thought it would be a long time before I could physically escape. Little did I know!

Following up on these experiences a bit, what I was doing is also called an "out of body experience" or "astral travel." Such experiences sometimes occur during surgery, when people feel themselves "floating" above or to the side of their physical bodies while under anesthesia. They see rather than feel what the doctors are doing to them. When these patients are being brought around after surgery, they feel as if they are being pulled back into their bodies. This also is the phenomena one feels in a near-death experience, in which one's "soul" separates from one's body and starts the journey one expects. One goes to the edge of that reality and gets a glimpse of "the other side."

First Escape!

Ed

When I was nine years old, I didn't know all the fancy jargon. I just knew I had found a way! I was determined to find the trigger that launched me into me into *that* reality. Innocence played a huge part in my ability to retain the skills. I didn't realize at the time how important this ability would be in my future life. It allowed me to escape. It played an integral part in an experience that occurred when I was eleven. My stepfather built a tractor from the frame and engine of a '49 Plymouth. We used to take it to the spring with a five-thousand-gallon tank and fill it for our drinking and cooking water for the week. As always, I was riding on back. We hit a bump, and I fell off and was thrown under the back wheels of the tractor. They ran over me and skidded down the entire length of my legs from hips down. My stepfather backed up and asked whether I was all right. I told him I didn't know. He told me that if I was still there when he got back with the water, he would pick me up and take me home. And off he drove, never checking me to see if I had broken anything. I was over 1.5 miles from home. Using my ability to escape within my mind, I was able to stumble my way home. I can't remember a time in my life before or since when I felt that much pain, both physical and emotional. My dad had left me in the middle of an old farm road, in the middle of the forest, over a mile from home! In my child's mind, I had come to know abandonment.

1959ish

Ed

I had learned that I could fly; that was life-changing! But the most system-shocking cultural shift in my life was to happen this year, and it turned into both a boon and a bane.

It started simply enough. A nice-looking couple stopped by our tobacco road habitation. They started a Bible study, and suddenly my parents found something *they* needed at the time—a totally immersive religious group. Suddenly, we were eating, sleeping, and breathing this religion.

Like most fundamentalist religious cult groups, we were discouraged to have any association with anyone outside the religion. We were stifled as to what entertainment was proper, and other such things. I was certainly not to talk about the kinds of experiences I was already having or the ones that I might soon be having. These were tantamount to worshiping Satan. If one was found to be in violation of any of the tenets of their teachings, one could be dis-fellowshipped or shunned, meaning separated from the congregation as well as from all friends and relatives within that faith. (Or, for those of the Catholic faith, it is like being excommunicated. For Catholics, this would mean not being able to participate in Communion.) It is not just this group that practices this barbaric custom. Many others in our world do as well.

My stepfather had climbed into a position of strength within the local hierarchy of the church, and as far as the ones just over him were concerned, he was golden. Most things he said or did were not questioned. One of the goals of this church was to preach in all out-of-the-way places. It was called "going where the need is great." My stepfather was sent into places to start groups and congregations. He and my mom were very successful in these activities. It got to be that my stepdad, who had never had any power since being in the army during WWII, was now in his glory. I saw him as one who was so bloated on his assumed strengths that they were sending him where the "great were needed."

Memories

Sonja

We made stop on Faial de Azores for refueling, and then flew on to Norfolk, Virginia. I don't know how it happened. I never heard many stories about that time. Children in those days were seen and not heard. One learned things only by being very, very quiet in shadowy spaces and praying that one never got caught. Some horrible punishment surely awaited the child who was so bold. I understood from the whispers of the elders who shadowed my young life that my mother had married an American soldier as some kind of trade. He had agreed to get us into the country. I understood that I did not have proper papers and had to remain unseen as much as possible. They separated soon after. All I can remember from those days is time in a motel room, going to the drive-in theater tucked into the backseat, my mother getting mad at me when I had to go potty in the middle of the show, sleeping between two overstuffed chairs made into a bed for me, and a young dark-haired man named Robert. I have no idea how much time passed. Common sense says that it must have been a few years, as I was an infant—too young to remember the flight.

My next memory is of walking down the sidewalk with my mom and seeing a sign above a doorway that read, "Martin's Photography Studio." I think I was about four. The first thing that fell out of my mouth was "Oh goody, we're home! And I even have my own room!"

My mother looked at me in horror. "Don't you say that! You don't know! People will think you're crazy! Don't you ever say that kind of lie again to anybody or you will get into big trouble!"

15

I was crushed. I could 'see' the room; it had pale green walls and pale-yellow kitchen cupboards. I "knew" it was my new home! It was the first inkling I had that there were things I could never talk about. I tried to be a big girl and not cry from the scolding. Not understanding my mom's quick anger or the fear in her eyes, I sniffled the shock deep inside. My mom went in to see whether they would hire her to do photography in their studio. She was quite good and had her own camera. We ended up with a small two-bedroom studio over the top of the store. It held a tiny kitchen and living room, a bathroom with a claw-foot tub, and two tiny bedrooms each about big enough for a single bed and dresser. The kitchen was the exact room I saw the first day I saw the studio sign.

I started repeatedly dreaming of a golden-haired man surrounded by waves. I drew pictures of the waves and boats, but the boats were always under the water. For some reason, I could never draw them on top of the water as they were supposed to be. I spent many days downstairs in the back of the studio where the owners lived, drawing all the time. I overheard the grown-ups saying that I should be outside. I understood that my constant drawing upset people, as they felt they might see something in my scribbles that would come true. I once said out of the blue, "I see Tippy, the dog, running away later." That afternoon, the dog found a way to leave the property! People freaked and were so upset. I had to watch everything I said. I nearly stopped talking. I didn't know what I could and could not say. I tried to draw houses, but the underwater boats kept leaking out of my crayons.

The owner's teenage daughter started taking me to the beach almost every day. (I think the adults wanted me out of the house because I creeped 'em out!) I remember the tar on the road being so hot! I asked whether they could really fry eggs on the road. I was told I was being silly. We had to walk on our towels to keep our feet from burning. I thought holding my towel and walking on the edges of it was the funniest thing I had ever heard of! I was always on watch for the golden-haired man and trying to figure out how boats could go underwater. I was puzzled by the dream, but what could I say? I was afraid to say the wrong thing. I didn't know what the wrong thing was. So when I was asked whether I had had any dreams, I would make up something silly like "Oh, I dreamed the chickens crossed the road." Everyone knew that that was not really my dream and that I was making it up. It seemed to be a kind of test to see whether I was having any more "seeing" dreams.

There were always whispers in the background. My "aunts" (elderly familial women) would whisper to my mom, "Don't let her do that. She will come to no good. If people find out she is a witch, it will ruin our business, and we won't be able to put our heads outside the door!"

My mother's father was a healer and physician in Stuttgart, Germany. In those days, that sort of thing was accepted and expected. He combined his traditional medical practice with laying-on-of-hands healing work and holistic ideas about breathing, good farm food, and sleeping outdoors in the winter to make your body healthy and strong. He believed that only clean, clear country air and water were good for you; that you always should breathe through your nose, not your mouth; and that every bite of food should be chewed twenty-four times. From what I understand, he was very psychic as well. My mother used to tell me stories of being punished when she got home from school because she had misbehaved in some way, and he had "seen" her activity. She grew up with very mixed feelings about healing. I'm sure that impacted our relationship with such things. The fear of being found out never left her.

My earliest memory of foresight is from when I was about four years old. I described to my mother her wedding: the dress she was wearing, the people that attended, and the kind of food that was served at lunch two weeks before she married my stepfather. I didn't know it was a wedding ceremony; I saw it as just a party. In those days, children were not told about such things. I was not aware that they were not yet married.

One day my mother and a man with golden hair went for a ride, and I was with them. I knew this was an important day because I was dressed in my Sunday best—black patent leather shoes and all! I was left in the car for a long time and remember that I got very hot, so I started taking off all my clothes. (I thought at the time it was pretty reasonable, since I could not open the car door.) When they came back, I was completely naked in the backseat! Now, common sense tells me that I must have met this man before, but other than my dreams, I have no memory of him whatsoever. After I was dressed and scolded—not in that order—I was told that this man was my new daddy. They had gone to city hall to get married. Years later I found out that he had been a sonar operator on a submarine in the US Navy. I found that interesting. Now I understood why the underwater boats kept leaking out of my crayons! Sometimes we may have insights that we can't place in a currently sensible way.

My dad had the gifts of "seeing" and hands-on healing. He became a police officer and worked in the state prison. He could calm down the most agitated prisoner by just putting his hand on the prisoner's shoulder. He knew before he got to a crash whether or not the people involved were alive or hurt. He could see the colors of their energy around them. He knew immediately if they were injured or not, in his head before he got to them and was able to call for the right kind of help before he even got there. Many of the other officers knew he had that ability, although no one talked openly about it. We talked about it now and then. He didn't think I was crazy but warned me to be careful about whom I shared this information with. I can remember stories he used to tell me about a women named Bridie Murphy. A book had been written about her. She lived a long time ago. One day she remembered a life that she had lived before. Research of the past, compared with the information she gave, proved at the time that it could be possible. I always thought the stories were interesting, and they opened a door for a different way of thinking.

We moved to a small white bungalow near the beach. I still had "seeing dreams" but often had no idea at the time what I was seeing. I certainly couldn't tell anyone about any dreams at all. I had dreamt that our little bungalow was painted with rainbow colors. I thought that was just beautiful! One day after Mom and Dad had finished painting rooms on the inside of the house, I found paint cans and brushes in the trash. I just picked them up and started painting as far up as my little arms could reach. I was so happy painting my little rainbow house. I so wanted to surprise my parents when they saw it. They came outside and saw my beautiful paint job and they were horrified! I was paddled, and as I was covered from head to foot with paint, I was scrubbed in turpentine to within an inch of my life to get off the paint off. My golden blond curls were shaved off, leaving me looking like a boy with a crew cut! I was never allowed to touch a paint brush again, ever. Even when I was a teenager, the story was brought up again and again in the family any time there was something to paint. I learned that even though I could "dream see," I could never know how accurately I was "seeing." I never knew what was whole, what was partial, what was missing, or what the ending was.

As time moved on, I became aware that other people didn't "see" things the way I did. I remember an uncle wanting to put me on his lap as a child. I didn't want to and started screaming because he kept insisting. I was punished and sent to my room for being so rude. But all I could see was dark around him. There were no colors, just darkness. He died of a massive heart attack the next day. I couldn't tell anyone what I had seen—or rather *not* seen. I didn't have the words to explain or the understanding that others couldn't see the things that I did.

In thinking of that incident years later, I began to wonder whether and how our lives are predetermined. If he had been paying attention, would he have known he was going to die? Could he have prevented it? If I could see such a change, why couldn't others? Maybe they did but they didn't know what they were seeing. I have learned now that most people see auras but don't know what they are seeing. Many "feel" the energy rather than see it. When we meet someone and know right away that he or she would make a good friend, or when we meet someone and feel like backing away, we are feeling aura energy. Most of us have not been taught that we can see as well as feel. Once we are shown how, we are amazed! Everyone expects bright colors and fireworks, but because they don't expect anything less, they miss the subtleties of the soft glow and soft waves of flowing energy.

Time Shifts

Time passed in the normal way. Day after day … step-by-step. The "eye dreams" came and slipped by. I didn't pay them a lot of mind now. They were just part of my nighttime life, as were other dreams of old men and owls, odd smells, and strange brown houses with trains going past them. I never told anyone anything more about my "dream seeing" and slowly forgot much of my nighttime life.

My parents and I eventually moved to Richfield Park, New Jersey. We lived in a small upstairs apartment next to a movie theater. The kitchen was painted institution green. My parents had a bedroom, and I slept on the sun porch, which was filled with glorious windows. I could see the stars at night and the sunrise in the morning. It was there that I saw my first praying mantis! I thought she was the most beautiful thing I had ever seen as the morning sun glinted off her pale green body! We had an overgrown, weed-filled, unattended backyard full of wild basil and straggling, unkempt tomato plants. I'm sure they were from kitchen scraps. The aroma was wonderful. I loved to roll around in the weeds, covering myself with the delightful smell. The yard was bounded by a large junk-filled ditch. I learned I could fly in the daytime there!

I knew I could fly at night. I could go anywhere. I don't know just when I started to realize I could fly. If I thought about flying as I was drifting off, I would rise up and out. It seemed I could always do this. I couldn't get to bed fast enough at night. I just wanted to go! Being sent to bed early as a punishment was a joy. I didn't mind, even if I couldn't have supper.

By day I ran and jumped as high as I could. I ran and jumped in circles round and round the yard, as fast and high as I could. Looking up at the sky, I would jump with all my strength, over and over. The grown-ups said I was crazy. They told my mother I needed other kids to play with. My mother did not agree. She said I would talk too much. I couldn't figure that out. I always tried so hard not to overtalk. (I eventually figured out that they weren't worried about my talking, but rather about what I might say!) I was alone a lot, but I didn't mind. I was too busy trying to figure things out. With no one to talk to, what's a curious flier to do? When I flew in my mind, I could see our apartment building, the street, and the roofs of the apartments on the other side of the street and those next door to us. I knew it was real because I could see stuff on the rooftops I could never have seen from the ground. I was so shocked when I realized I was flying that I collapsed on the ground. I was never able to do it again, although I tried; God knows I tried. It was many years before I learned about astral flight and many years before I left my body again, fully conscious. But I could always fly when I was asleep.

In later life, I took flying lessons in a real plane—a Piper Cub! I came within a hair's breadth of getting my pilot's license. Life intervened and had a different plan for me. I was crushed at the time. My goal was to fly solo across the country. I knew it had been done already, so it was not a big deal for others, but it was for me! My dreams said it was so! In my dreams, I was just flying and flying, looking out the window and seeing the ant-sized people and toylike cars below, and the clouds surrounding me. Circular rainbows were always flying along with the plane. Few people see them, but I knew I would.

I was so angry and upset when things didn't work out the way I thought they were supposed to. I had put lots of time, money, and study into learning everything just right. I intended to be the best and most trusted pilot. I had put every penny I had into paying for the lessons. I wanted to fly like my dad. He used to take me flying with him now and then when I was a child, and sometimes he even let me touch the controls! I'm sure I didn't really fly anything when he did that; he was just a dad being a dad. I don't think at my vintage age I can get a pilot's license now. If I could, you bet I would! But I think my next goal is skydiving! Yep, I think jumping from a plane would be the hottest thing! Anyone want to take me up? I'm ready!

Da Da

One of my best memories as a child is that of going with my parents down into the bowels of a five-story walk-up, down a long corridor, way to the back, and into a large room. There was a bulkhead door leading to daylight outside. It was Frank Delatoe's home. It was spooky but full of possibilities for an imaginative child. There were laundry lines hung catty-corner in one part of the room filled with men's sleeveless T-shirts. The walls were brick with mortar that had pooched out around their edges long ago.

The cellar guy was dark, dank, and old-man smelly. But he made the best spaghetti! I got to sit with the grown-ups in the shadowy room lit with several kerosene lamps at the wobbly card table and drink tiny glasses of sherry. (I didn't know it was sherry until I grew up and had some and remembered the taste.) They would talk, play cards, and smoke. My mother would laugh her sultry laugh. She was made up as if they were going to the opera. My dad was a sharp dresser as well, even to go to the cellar. They drank and smoked way into the early morning. I was happily sitting on the tattered old sofa, wrapped in my blankie, sipping sherry, dreaming into the flickering light, and watching prophetic pictures dance on the walls as I was nodding off. Adult words shifted through the shadows of the sherry. Phantom words slipped in between my half-asleep brain and the sips of sherry. They sounded like "guest," "father," "upstairs" … As the adults continued to chat together, I felt fuzzy words slip by with partially formed pictures, but I could not make them out. I wondered, as I was being carried up the steps, what they would turn into. I could feel the words forming pictures that I could almost see, with trails of half-words skipping by, out of sight, to the hidden spaces of

24

my brain. I remember how the sunrise looked from my father's shoulder as he carried me up the steps to home. I remember feeling peaceful.

Eventually we moved to a three-story home in Hackensack, New Jersey, that stood across from a car dealership and a railroad track. Three of my brothers were born there, and several years later, a sister.

My grandfather, from Denmark, moved in with us. I had been expecting him for months. Well, not him, exactly. But seeing smoke rings in the living room as well as smelling delicious White Owl cigar smoke every now and then announced his coming arrival. The sights and smells just made me tingle all over with anticipation. I didn't know what I was smelling or seeing. I had never seen a cigar ring or know the difference between the smell of the Lucky Strikes my parents smoked and the richness of a White Owl cigar. I knew the day he moved in with little fanfare that he was the "expected one." His clothing was woolen, proper, and gentlemanly. A light aroma of good tobacco lingered as he moved through the house. He was a quiet, mysterious man with sparkling blue eyes just like his son's. He had white hair, was old-school, and spoke in a soft, heavy voice. I loved him immediately and knew he would be an ally.

He had come from Denmark, where his parents had owned a chocolate factory. His family had settled in Westbrook, Maine, and New Jersey. Years prior, his wife had died in childbirth, leaving him with his only son, my stepfather, who had been born in American waters off the coast of New Jersey.

My father was raised in Westbrook, Maine. He lived with relatives during his school years. His father could not care for him, as he had to work. After my parents married, his dad, my dada, came to live with us for all the years we lived in New Jersey, gracing us with his knowing eyes and deep Danish accent. After a few weeks, he got a job as a butter taster at a creamery in New York. Every now and then, he would take me to work with him and we would ride the ferry across to the city. I loved standing on the rolling deck, feeling the wind and water in my face as the seagulls flew overhead, scolding us for interrupting their day. Sunday morning at 6:00 a.m. sharp, he would walk to the bakery, and every Sunday morning we would have warm, fresh bakery rolls sprinkled with poppy seeds and spread with fresh creamery butter. I was allowed to have "coffee milk" on Sunday mornings made with about a quarter cup of real coffee, sugar, and a cup full of milk. I drank it from a coffee cup just like the grown-ups.

Dada, as we called him, was given my room on the third floor, and I was put down with the boys on the second floor. The boys, Jason, Jeff, and Bobbie were in the same room. I had a small room of my own because I was the only girl so far. They were a handful. Four-year-old Jason would regularly tie a sheet around his neck and stand on the windowsill, threatening to fly like Superman, causing our parents to put bars on the second-story window. Jeff was a quiet child on the surface but continually goaded Jason into doing devilish and exciting things—which, of course, Jason always got in trouble for. No one cared when he insisted, "Jeff made me do it!" Bobbie was a baby and didn't get into much trouble at the time.

I had my own room between the boys and my parents. My mother, who worked very hard to be, in her words, a "successful American woman", became president of the local PTA. She was a stylish and sought-after interior decorator who was well-known for her upper class European entertaining. She had a beautiful style not seen in the area before. My father owned a gas station at the time. Their idea of lifestyle and finances did not fit into the same picture. My mother was tough and strict with a family history of "in her words" some bit of German royalty." Her family was wealthy before the war. When times got difficult in our family, she became a taxi driver in New York City, working under the cover of night so the neighbors wouldn't know. She was a tough bird in many ways. When my brother Jason was born, she had been driving her route in the city when she went into labor. She pulled into a hospital in the middle of the night, delivered Jason, and was back on her route for her morning run, never missing a beat! (Years later, she became the first woman Maine hunting guide, as well as the first woman real estate broker in the State of Maine to have her own business. She also ran her own hunting camp for many years. She was tough!)

Being so close to my parents at night brought sounds that were no longer muffled to my ears. It was many years before I understood what alcoholism was and how it can erode the very life out of someone. I missed my old room in the peak of the house. I was alone there, away from prying eyes and ears, where I could hold conversations with the children and animals who lived in the quiet spaces. I could see marvels in my universe that no one else would admit to. I could see far across the city as the full moon cast shimmering shadows on my wall. Rooflines, chimneys, and TV antennas in twilight shadows were like another world.

My grandfather came into my room one evening as I was softly speaking to the unseen visitors around me. I jumped when I heard my door open. His large softness filled the room. He gazed at me for a moment, and I held my breath, wondering what he might have heard and whether I would be punished. He looked around the room and gave a short nod and wink of his eye as he slowly backed out, shutting my door behind him. I knew immediately that he knew what I had been doing! We never talked about it, but I knew he had the seeing dreams too! That was all I needed—an ally. We never spoke of it, but each of us knowing that the other knew would always be our secret. My heart was happy even though I knew we must never talk about it. I was so filled with joy that this beloved man could see who I really was.

During winters in those days, we would make the long trip to Westbrook, Maine, to spend Christmas week with Dada's brother and his wife. It was proper old Europe. Children were not to speak unless spoken to, at any time. If we wanted to speak, we stood with our hands behind our backs until we were acknowledged by an adult and asked what we wanted. We ate what was on our plates, or we went without. We used our napkins and did not ever pick up food with our fingers—not even fried chicken. We did not ask for seconds but waited for them to be offered. Leaving even a scrap of food on one's plate was considered a breach of etiquette. After all, there were starving children in China! Most of the time, we dared not take seconds lest we leave some scrap, meaning that punishment would rain upon us later.

As the oldest, I was expected to keep the younger ones in line. "Please" and "thank you" went without question. I dared not miss even one. We hardly relaxed or played around the adults because our parents would give us the eye, and we knew better than to even make a squeak out of place. I was a nervous wreck during these visits. My brother Jason would always try some new adventure, such as trying to climb up the chimney from the inside of the fireplace when no one was watching and get me into trouble. Or Jeff would poke Jason to make him scream. (Guess who was charged with keeping them quiet?) I felt like the Royal Guard, at attentionat all times. The only relief I had was at night. The dark was my friend. As soon as I heard the soft sleeping breath of the little ones, I was free to fly away. Through the ceiling I would go, and then over the rooftops, swooping across the snowbound countryside. There I found peace and freedom.

Life Changes

When I was about nine, we moved to Maine. My parents had fallen into financial difficulties and lost our home. Dada stayed in the city. We moved into a world that could have been on a different planet.

There was no electricity or water in the house, and no indoor plumbing. Chickens and cows wandered in the yard. Amazingly, I never saw it coming. I was as shocked as the rest of the kids. Not "seeing" something that important made me wonder how I could trust something I could not be sure of. How could I not have known? Maybe I really was crazy. I had not had even an inkling!

Life in the country was shockingly different for us. There were acres of fields and woods for us to roam in. There was no city noise. I was scared of the quiet at first, and I then realized that there was a beautiful cornucopia of sounds surrounding me and I could understand the language of the wind, leaves rustling, and critters around chattering. I got it! I could figure out the weather by what the wild was doing around me. I never knew people could do that.

The house was strange; it smelled like old, wet dog. The people before us had raised hunting dogs inside. Talk about old, wet dog hair! Ugh! We had no indoor plumbing. We got used to the three-seater outhouse. I never understood why it was called an outhouse. I thought it should have been called a "poop house," as it stank! There was no running water inside, but there was an old hand pump in the yard that connected to a well. I learned the hard way that it took twenty pails of cold water from the well pump to do a load of laundry in the wringer washer, and another six pails for a bath in the tub, which was placed in front of the wood stove in the winter. We all used the same water; we just added more from the kettle atop the wood stove, where it had been simmering. Little ones went first, a couple at a time, and then the next oldest, and so forth. As the girls got older, the bath water was changed between girls' and boys' turns. The water from our well tasted like liquid sun! I had never had real, untreated water in my life. It was amazing. I still can't forget the sweetness of it.

In summer, we all went swimming in the farm pond. Big kids watched the little ones. Mud, slippery frogs, and all, it was slippery fun!

Darkness

I started having dreams of dark clouds swallowing me up. The "Dark One" came often. Sometimes it looked like small, dark kitten feet; they quietly covered each rustle of the tiniest leaves so I would never know it was coming until it was too late. Then it was so dark and quiet that I felt as if I wasn't there at all. At times, the dark spread its blackness like a Rorschach test over a white blotter in frightening shapes that I had never seen before, coming closer and closer to cover me. Sometimes it was like shards of dark glass breaking away from the starry heavens, shattering as they fell. They always came. I would wake up screaming in the middle of the night, stuffing my streaming wet face into my pillow. My beloved daddy was gone. I was so afraid. I woke sobbing night after night. Dada had died and gone into an unreachable shadow world. I was alone. Darkness and horror covered me. I was being chased by blackness. My life was about to take a dramatic turn. Gone were the pleasing and exciting shadow visions of stars, sunlight, and brilliant, loving blue eyes. Gone for many years …

By age eleven, I had adjusted to country life. I was running through freshly cut hay fields barefoot, gliding with the ease of a mountain snowshoer on the golden stubble, and climbing to the top of the hundred-year-old maple in the yard, pretending I was Tarzan. I couldn't stand the simpering Jane. I herded my goats over the bramble-covered New England rock walls. My bare feet hugged the warm sun-kissed rocks as I made my way across, though, and over the sultry land. We couldn't afford shoes in the summer. The boys worked all summer hauling wood with no shoes. It was hard man's work, even though they were just kids. Sometimes they got lucky and had some sneakers given to them. They wore them until there were only soles left and would sometimes tie the tattered soles onto their feet to give them some protection. Sometimes in winter they wore plastic bread bags over their holey socks, held up with canning jar rubbers inside their gum rubber boots. We always joked that we didn't have to go to church because our socks were already "holy"!

Our father was gone a lot. He worked for the Bangor & Aroostock Railroad at that time.

When our parents eventually got divorced, mom hired a young mountain man to help with the farm work.

I had been having the dark dreams for what seemed like forever. Now they occurred nearly every night. Once, I had found such solace in the night, but even my night peace had gone now.

The mountain man had been there most of the time while Dad was gone, so we knew him and thought he was a friend; we knew he was mom's best friend. He was always nice to us, giving us extra rides on the tractor or into town when mom wasn't home; slipping us a piece of mom's chocolate candy that we were not supposed to have; or letting us stay up late if she was at a meeting, as long as it we promised not to tell. He told us it would be just our little secret. We giggled, enjoying our private, secret little kind of grown-up game. We were innocent in the truest sense of the word. We watched *Disneyland* on TV on Sundays, and we listened to C & W on the radio when we were allowed. We did not see many outsiders at that time. He moved in with us, even though he was a drifter type. He had long hair, was not so clean, and smelled like beer and sweat. He smoked the funniest cigarettes I had ever seen. He "rolled his own." I didn't know people did that. I had always seen my parents smoking Lucky Strikes or Camels. He was twenty years my mother's junior. He had eyes for the girls and the boys alike—even his children, who were born over the years. Our lives became a living nightmare. The first time I saw him drunk, it terrified me. I had never seen anyone so out of control and acting so loud and crazy.

Our mother would never believe us, from the baby to the older ones. Age never mattered. I couldn't fix it. I couldn't fix it for them. I couldn't fix it for me. As the oldest, it was my job to keep them safe. The feelings of uselessness were overwhelming. I considered leaving—rising up and just letting myself go, flying away into the stars and never coming back. Or just walking into the woods with my rifle. But I couldn't leave them. It was during those times that I started to embroider my words into intricate colored patterns, even if they never left the deep purple of my mind. I could not write openly, lest someone find my words. What I dared to write was in code so no one would ever find out.

Things were bad. One day one of the younger ones came in crying. When I asked what was wrong, she blurted out that the "dark one" had hurt her. When I pushed a bit more, a story unfolded that even at my young age I knew could only be the truth. She would otherwise have had no concept of the tale she told me at eight years old. She was specific. She could not have made it up. I decided I would take the situation into hand.

At sixteen, I was already a crack shot. We lived in the woods and hunted our food or grew it. The hunting law was that you had to be ten years old and be with an adult. The boys hunted much more than I did—even at a younger age, but in the country, who knew? We all learned as soon as we were old enough. We were taught early to only make clean kills; if we could not be certain of a clean kill, we were not to try. We were taught gun safety in high school when we got there, and we aced the classes!

I decided to take care of the situation. I planned it out. I felt I could stage it as an accident. I was mulling it over to make sure my plan would work. One night I had a dream. An angel came in my dream. His name was Cameron. Even though it freaked me out, I never forgot, and he never came again. He said, "Don't do it. You will be found out. Everyone knows you are a great shot. No one will believe it was an accident. You know too much about the woods. There are many more than you think who know the truth but will not speak up because they are in it, and you will be found out. You will do better things if you stay here as long as your time is for here."

I was shaken up for days, but in the end, it made sense. So, I tried to be always vigilant. During those days, if you were a family member, you could not report such goings on. Only someone from outside would be believed or be able to file charges. It was thought that a family member might have something against the person accused and could be trying to start trouble. I went to the state police, and that's what I was told. No one else would step up. Years later, when the kids grew up, I learned the horrible truth of who had known everything about the girls and boys, as well as who had been involved. It broke my heart. I had no idea that such evil existed. At that point, there was nothing I could do.

Light Shines in Mysterious Ways at Times

The boy came to the house one day with his parents who were missionaries. He was a gangly blond-haired, blue-eyed shy boy with funny long toes who was near my age. *City kid*, I thought. He didn't say much. He was more of a curiosity than anything else. He had scared blue eyes, not the ones of my dreams. He hardly said a word for weeks during the adult Bible classes.

I decided I liked him. He was quiet. He listened to me and really heard me. He didn't do the "boy thing." You know, like my pesky brothers! I had five brothers at the time. I didn't need another boy child to tend to. His eyes were not the eyes in my dreams, but there was something—a twinkle, a laughter behind sadness, or a hidden rascal, maybe. This was a boy who could fly with me through the winds, scamper across the rocks to catch the goats, and climb trees as well as I could and not give me grief about being a tomboy … maybe.

Harvard and his family came over each week for Bible study. During the adult portion, he and I would sit on the front lawn after the little kids went to bed. He was always helpful. I thought it odd that this boy who had no siblings would want to help me get them all to bed and was so thoughtful and good about how to do it. There were five of them now, and they could be a handful at times. When we were done and the little ones were down and quiet, we were allowed to sit on the front lawn together as long as we were in sight of the front door and the living room windows. We sat and talked about the strangest things:

"Do you think other people live on the stars?"

"Can you see the fairy people too?"

"Where do you think we come from?"

"Yes, I saw some little people in the woods."

"Yes, I think there must be people up there someplace."

"I don't know where we came from … maybe we just got planted or just got dropped off here somehow."

The conversations went on for many weeks in the summer. Back in those long-ago days, summer was always at least six months long! The soft aroma of the new grass gave way to the biting black flies and then the incredible, spirited lightning bugs. We caught them and put them in jars. The younger kids were allowed to stay up late some nights and catch lightning bugs with us. The they would each have a jar of them to take to bed. They understood they had to let them go in the morning.

Sometimes Harvey was allowed to come over during the day during raspberry-picking time in the summer. I was happy to see him but had to act as if it was no big deal. But underneath my shirt, my heart was racing like a runaway train! He was my only friend. To have a friend my age was truly amazing, even if he was a boy! I was not allowed to have friends over or go visit them off property. (There was too much of a chance of people finding out the truth of what was really going on in our home..)

Raspberries

Down the trail on the way to the timber slash where the raspberries grew was a huge rock covered with moss. Next to it was a deep depression that filled with water. This was a fantastic place for pollywogs to skip around the reeds and cattails that grew on the edges. I often saw bits of color flashing around the area. I thought at first there was something wrong with my eyes, but then I realized, *Oh, it's the fairy people! Amazing, I can see them! I wonder if they can see me?* I couldn't say anything. People already thought I was odd, and some said I was crazy or a witch, so I never told anyone but Harvey. He said he could see them too and that he could see other things as well. But he would never tell me what he saw. We usually took the kids by the "fairy rock" and let them rest for a bit before starting out.

It was high summer. I could hear the high-pitched buzz of the heat bugs as soon as I stepped out of the house. I have no idea what they were really called. We just knew that when the temperature was just right, you would start hearing them in the high summer, just about raspberry-picking time.

That was one of the jobs us kids had—picking raspberries as soon as they were ripe. The season would last only a couple of weeks, maybe, if there was no heavy rain to ruin them. Once the berries were picked, it was time to make jam for winter. The best berries were boxed up to sell to Knox Berry Farm in Belfast. (Not the famous one) It was a scramble to get ready right after breakfast and after the dew had evaporated. Packing a lunch for five healthy boys, me, and the baby could be frustrating at the time, as each one said what kind of a lunch he or she wanted. We didn't have a choice. They knew it. They just liked to give me a hard time.

Sometimes Harvey—today known as Fuzz—would be allowed to come with us. He was a big help, especially with the little one. He would help carry her so I could pick and keep an eye on those rascally brothers. He was the only one who had shoes. He was not a barefoot kind of kid. Once, I saw him in his bare feet and thought he had the funniest long toes. We laugh about it even today. Our family all have short toes.

In the picnic basket went peanut butter and grape jelly sandwiches or tuna sandwiches with everything under the sun in them. One can of tuna had to go a long way. The bread we used was homemade bread or biscuits I had made the day before. We also brought a jug of orange Kool-aid, a bottle for the youngest, and an extra diaper or two. There were no pampers in those days. Each of us had a pail—either a plastic peanut butter pail or a tin pail from who knows where. The rule was that the pails had to be filled and there was to be *no eating!* (Of course, there was. Well, some. But no one would tell. We made sure our tongues and teeth were totally clean before we got back home.) Our mother would check our mouths!

Off we went down the trail through the ancient apple orchard that hadn't been cared for in years. Sometimes we made a short stop in the orchard to say hello to Chippie the Chipmunk. We liked to believe that he knew who we were and that he liked that we would leave bits of food around for him. Through the elderly unkempt orchard we went, on through the woodland pathways to the timber slash. Around the pathways were beech trees, pines, and assorted hardwoods. The woods trail was filled with the sweet aromas of living and blossoming plants as well as the moldy, leafy softness of old wood becoming earth again. Birds, squirrels, rabbits, and chipmunks would jump out when we least expected. Sometimes we thought that maybe we could catch one as a pet!

The timber slash was a place in the woods that had been harvested for timber and pulp years before, and the leavings had been just left. Wild raspberries hung heavily on low bending canes. We clambered over the logs with their soft, cool moss covering the tops, the bottoms of our bare feet thankfully sinking in as deep as the moss would allow. The cool softness felt so good. The morning of picking was filled with the voices of kids' chatter. Someone would yell, "He's eating one!" or "I'm telling Mom!" or "I saw a deer!" In the latter case, we would look up and see a whitetail bounding cleanly over the downed and rotting logs off into the brush.

The boys would start talking about hunting in the fall and how they would remember just where the deer trails were. I would put the baby on a patch of moss with her bottle and the lunch basket and would go on picking berries. We had to hurry to get our pails filled and get home before the afternoon heat hit. The heat would turn the berries into mush that would sink into the bottoms of our pails. With mushy berries, we would never get our pails filled; nor could they be sold. So, the rush was on.

Guardians of the Woods: Light in Our Summer

Berry picking was hard work, especially with so many kids to look after. So, one day we decided to take a break from the work, thinking that if they could rest a while, it would be easier for everyone. So in the cool of the morning, we gathered them around the huge boulder we called the fairy rock and told them a story that was pretty much based on truth (the key here being the "pretty much" part.) We had the gift of seeing the bits of fairy color dancing in the light or hiding behind the trees as we passed ... And if we sat very still, kind of looking sideways, they would speak to us.

How Birds' Nests Came To Be

A long, long time ago, far away in the deep woods, there lived a family of towheaded children. (This meant their hair was very blond, almost white—the color of newly spun flax. People called us the towhead kids, even though some of us had darker hair.)

The towheaded kids lived in the deep woods. They were very poor and rarely saw other people and never, ever left the deep wood except to go to school. They had to walk through the forest and down a long dirt path to get to their little one-room schoolhouse (with thirty-eight kids, one teacher, and eight grades!).

In the winter, they could take their long wooden sled, called a toboggan, and slide all the way to school. The toboggan was so big that all six children could fit on at one time. Jason always got to ride in front of the two little girls, Sally and Jackie. Then came the rest of the boys. The two little ones, Dick and Jacob, were next, with the second-oldest, Jeff, in the back so the little ones wouldn't fall off.

In the summertime, the children worked very hard. The boys worked in the woods cutting trees and moving brush. The girls worked in the many gardens, planting, weeding, and harvesting to get food ready for winter.

The children were often hungry. Even though there were plenty of good, fresh vegetables in the gardens, much of the time the grown-ups would not allow the children to eat unless all the work was done. Sometimes the children were just too tired to stay awake for supper and went to bed hungry. In the morning, the children would have oatmeal for breakfast. Sometimes the oatmeal was burned. All of the children hated burnt oatmeal, but if they didn't eat it, they could have nothing else to eat for the rest of the day.

During high summer, the forest came alive with birds and flowers and all manner of wild berries. All of the children, even the smallest one, would be sent forth into the deepest part of the forest to pick raspberries. The berries would be made into jam for the winter and sold to the market.

The children were told not to come home until all their baskets and pails were filled to the top! Day after day during the short season, the children trudged hungrily through the woods to find the best berries, hoping to fill their baskets quickly and return home.

One night the oldest sister, whose nickname was Sunny, had a dream. In the dream she saw the "Guardians of the Woods," the fairies, dancing on moss around the fairy rock by the tiny pond in the deep woods. In the dream, the queen fairy said to her, "We love little children. Please bring them to the fairy rock tomorrow on your way to pick berries. We have a surprise for you." Sunny woke up with a start, thinking what a silly dream she had had. She had dreamt of fairies many times before, and sometimes she even saw them in broad daylight. But no one ever believed her.

But this day she gathered up the children as they headed for the deep woods and told them she had a special surprise for them. They were so excited there was going to be a surprise! Oh! What could it be? New shoes, some special food? A piece of candy, maybe?

Sunny told them they had to be very, very quiet and follow her without saying a peep until they reached the fairy rock. The bigger children held the hands of the little ones, and they all held their berry buckets close to their chests so as not to make any creaking sounds.

As the children were seated in a quiet circle around the fairy rock (they could be very well-behaved children when they wanted to be!), little brightly colored flying things began flitting around them. Sunny looked with wide eyes. *Fairies! Oh my, fairies! They are really here, and the children can see them too!*

The children started to giggle and laugh as the little bits of color tickled their noses and frolicked on their heads, darted in front of their wide-open eyes, and did loops in the air!

After such an attention-getting introduction, the tiny fairy people settled on top of the fairy rock. Some sat on swinging blades of grass around the tiny fairy pond, and one or two flew up into the tree's branches to get a better view.

Suddenly the forest, which had just been teeming with life and laughter, became so quiet one could hear a leaf drop!

Out of thin air, the queen fairy appeared before them. She was beautiful in her sky-blue gown, her hair flaming red. Her golden gossamer wings were fluttering, holding her in midair as if by magic.

"Children," she said in her tiny voice, "we have been watching you every day. We are so happy that you take such good care of our home. We see that you are careful not to step on any flowering plants, that you are quiet so as not to frighten the little forest animals, and that you leave the pathways as clean as you found them. Because we know that you are very good children, we will grant you one wish."

The children started to whisper among themselves. Only one wish—what would it be? Candy? New shoes? No more school? No more work? No more oatmeal? Wait! That was it! Something good for breakfast. Little Sally, the most towheaded one (which she still is to this very day!) was chosen to speak for all the children.

Scooching down to make herself even smaller (so as not to frighten the queen fairy, you know), Little Sally said, "Queen Fairy, if you please, we would like something different for breakfast."

The queen looked at the sweet little child with a warm gaze and asked, "My dear, what would you like that to be?" Just as Sally started to open her small mouth to speak, Bobby jumped to his feet, pointed to a partly hidden tree branch (nearly knocking a fairy into the next world, I might add), and yelled, "Bird's nest! Oh! Look, I found a bird's nest!" A shocked hush fell over the little group as the queen fairy said, "So be it. Your wish has been granted! Whenever you want a special treat for your breakfast, you shall have birds' nests!"

The fairy people giggled and danced. They did loops and clapped their hands and sang for all to hear, for fay people are full of fun and frolic and, at times, a bit of mischief.

The children were bewildered at such happenings. But Sunny said to them, "Oh, don't you see? It's a riddle. We won't have to eat a *real* bird's nest! Let's all think really hard about birds' nests and see what we can come up with."

As the children went about their day of berry-picking, they thought and talked about birds' nests and how they were made, whether people could really eat them, and so on. The day went so fast; the buckets were filled in no time.

That night, as Sunny was sleeping, the queen fairy came to her in a dream and whispered the magic recipe for the children's special breakfast. Sunny got up early in the morning, collected the eggs from the chickens, and sliced the fresh homemade bread.

Lo and behold, when the children came down for their morning meal, they found beautiful golden-brown birds' nests on their plates! They were so happy. From that day forward, birds' nests were always served in our family when a child wanted a special treat for breakfast.

And just so you know, in case you're wondering what happened to the grown-ups, the good fairies made sure they sprinkled an extra measure of sleeping dust on them so that they slept far into the day.

When Sunny grew up and had children of her own, she told them this fairy story and taught them how to make birds' nests. Her children have taught their children, and so it goes.

Birds' nests are simple fare: a slice of bread—any kind. Cut a hole in the center with a glass or small cookie cutter. Butter both sides of the bread and the center piece. Put the bread in a frying pan or on a griddle and break an egg into each hole. Cook one side and then the other. Do the same for the center piece.

~~~~~~~~~~~~~~

Years later, I read the story of Edgar Cacey, America's sleeping prophet, and for the first time I realized others saw fairies too. I wasn't crazy after all. He passed in 1945. The Edgar Cacey Foundation is located in Norfolk, Virginia.

Healing Hands

It seems that whenever anyone, my brothers or the woodsmen, came in with an injury, I always was the one to get the bandages or the Epsom salts to soak a wound, an injured foot, or what have you. I kept dried puffballs in my first aid kit as well as in the bathroom cupboard. Puffballs are mushrooms that grow wild; their dried spores help stop bleeding. I don't know the names of the different types of puffballs; I only know what they look like, and I always picked bunches after they dried naturally. I would gather enough for the following year, since I could only pick them when they were ready. I never had a problem with blood and guts, whereas my mother would faint. There was a lot of talk of my "healing hands." It got so my stepfather's mother, Nana, would come whenever she had a "sick headache" (migraine) and ask me to put my hands on her head. She said it was the only thing that would touch the pain. After a while, people started dropping by the house, asking me to put my hands on their arthritic knees and such. Each time I put my hands on someone I could "see" whether the situation was getting better or not. My mother always tried to downplay the situation and the attention. Early in my adult life, I focused on healing energy. I used it without understanding what it really was or where it came from in the beginning.

I often knew what was in a letter before it was opened, and I always knew what was happening at home before I got there. (Both of my parents were into the "cup, papers, and pipe" more than a little. My foresight saved me from many beatings and punishments. Before I got there, I would "know" what to say or how to act when I got home so as not to upset anyone.)

My mother changed religions as most women changed hats in those days, dragging us along behind. I was "born" Catholic. When I came to this country, I "became" Lutheran. When we moved to Maine, I attended the local Baptist church, then a Methodist church, a Congregationalist church, the Church of the Nazarene, a Pentecostal church, and others. The church elders convinced my mother that I was working with the devil. Someone had seen me feeding a wild bear out of my hand and had heard rumors about me picking up an injured raccoon without injury to myself. (I had grown up around animals both wild and domesticated, I honestly never thought they would hurt me; we lived in the woods and didn't think anything of it. I was just helping them.) I had started to freak people out. My mother lowered the boom, and I was constantly watched for any unusual behavior, such as working with injured animals, letting a bird land on my arm, or attending to the household injuries of my siblings. She did not want to be embarrassed by having a "crazy child." The good from all these changes was that it gave me a much broader, more open view of how others believed in different things and had different ways of responding to the Creator.

I learned to keep quiet; I think this was because I couldn't understand how so many groups were so different but almost the same. I never knew what the right or wrong thing was to say or do. That was about the same time I decided, in my childish mind, that Jesus Christ was just an intermediary and that if God was real, there was no reason that I, as a child of God, couldn't go right to the top with my prayers and questions. I knew in my heart that I was good and that the grown-ups didn't know what they were talking about, so why couldn't I just go to the Father and not worry about the Son? It made sense to me at that age.

This was also the time frame during which I met Ed.

Love of My Life

Ed

A couple of months later, we moved to Liberty, Maine. During the time that my parents were doing missionary work, they came to a farmhouse on the top of a hill and started a Bible study with the man and woman who lived there. The woman had seven children at the time. I was an only child. This whole town in one house intrigued me. The oldest child was a honey-blonde girl who had the most wonderful smile and sparkling laugh you ever heard. We were both around ten or eleven when we met. I have been in love with her since that day.

We would spend the evenings together with her brothers and sisters out on the lawn during the adult part of the Bible class. When it was time to put them to bed, I helped her as much as I could, never having been around small children before. Once they were snuggled into their beds, we could talk about all manner of strange things. We'd listen to the droning of the adults talking as we watched the most wonderful light show known to humankind: the dark velvet night, with its millions of points of light quivering like birthday candles on an inverted cake. The Milky Way frothed along its ribbed path as all of the stars wheeled across the sky. We both had some unusual experiences. We wondered as time went by who we were, why we were here, and where we came from—questions every child has. Maybe it was childish dreaming. But we both felt a kinship to the stars and felt that we were indeed from one of those points of light. Then it was just a matter of trying to figure out which one. I always had an affinity for Orion and came to believe that was where I was from. I felt that maybe we both came from the third star in his belt.

We did some childish things in those days. We would blink an SOS signal with our flashlight to the stars, hoping our "real" parents would come and collect us from this strange place and take us back to our gardens and star fields.

Innocents

The days went on, with two innocents flying and exploring their universe of micro and macro, light filling each vibration. Yes, they knew some of the world, but to them it had not become real or solid yet. They were too young. They knew only love for the earth and all that surrounded them. Their light filled each cell.

During the four to five yearswe were friends, we learned of many wonderful things, mostly by experience. We discovered fairy circles, physical and mental commutation skills, and dream walking. Those experiences whetted our appetites to learn more. After we unexpectedly parted ways at fourteen, we both became seekers.

Starry, Starry Night

Sonja

The morning sun is dancing its sunbeams through my bedroom window, making dust particles pirouette and scamper in the morning light. It's Wednesday! I love Wednesday! Up and at 'em, get my chores done, tend to the little ones, and don't fuss about anything at all, all day! Tonight, is Bible study! I can't wait. I'm so very happy; I dance a little jig that no one can see but me! It's Wednesday! Whoopee!

Now the plan. I've got to have a plan. Get the kids fed and dressed and don't let them fuss. If they do, I'll be the one to get in trouble for not doing something right. So no yelling at them; only be nice—but not too nice. (It's Wednesday. A little happy dance escapes from my feet! Please don't see my happy, happy face with its twinkling eyes!) If those boys figure out that I'm happy about Wednesday, they will figure out why, and I will never hear the end of it, and the parents will find out! Oh God, please not that!

As the sun keeps its appointed rounds across the heavens, the day drags slowly on. I somehow get my chores done, keep the kids calm, and do everything just right with no one finding out. As the day slogs along, I try so hard to be so very good. It would not be good to be punished by being sent to bed early like a child.

Evening arrives at long last. Supper is done; the boys helped with the dishes. A little bribery goes a long way! I made sure every scrap of everything was picked up and cleared, keeping one eye on the kitchen clock. Dessert and coffee were put aside for the adults later. They are never late. The car should be driving up any minute.

The sun slips down behind the horizon at last. The parents are busy with their Bible study. He politely helps me put the little kids to bed. The older boys are allowed to stay up a while and play in their rooms if they promise to be quiet. The bright blue sky of the day has turned into a dark velvet night with millions of points of light quivering like billions of fireflies, the Milky Way frothing along its ribboned path. We settle on the damp grass of the front lawn as pale flickering lights dance through the old glass windows from within. We sit in plain sight of any adults who might care to look. Two hands shyly almost touch as the moist aroma of fresh grass washes over us while we sit on the lawn staring in wonder at the universe around us, asking again, "Where did we come from, and why are we here?" We are elevenish.

Blue Velvet Dreams

Sonja

It was another night filled with stars trying to lift us to their height, so magnificent above the earth, wanting to dance with us and fill us with their sweet night songs, the Milky Way waving for us to follow along its magical path.

Two hands were almost touching as the moist aroma of fresh grass washed over us as we sat together in the field, staring in wonder at the universe around us, still asking, "Where did we come from, and why are we here?"

The dreams were always. I never knew a time when they were not. From my earliest memory, it was always the loving blue eyes—kind, soft, loving, full, deep, safe blue eyes. No matter what dream came, the end was always the eyes. They haunted me. I peeked at everyone from afar, so as not to be found wanting, so as not to be misunderstood. I was always searching for the eyes, always—but never finding them. Were they only a figment? Were they real, were they talking to me? Would I ever find them?

Broken Heart

Ed,

My folks had decided to go back to Connecticut, in the summer of '56, so what was a fourteen-year-old to do? I had to go with them, so with my dear Sonja growing smaller in the rear window and the tears blurring my sight, I was whisked off to Bridgeport, Connecticut. My first experience with culture shock was about to start. First off, fairy circles are harder to find in the city!

The Hamburger Date

Sonja

My last memories of him were a tear-filled little face in the back window of the green 1952 Plymouth.

It had been nearly four years when I again recognized an older well-dressed man with a limp; a properly dressed white-haired, sweet-looking older lady; and a tall, nicely dressed man coming to the door. I recognized them immediately. I was excited, as I hadn't seen them in so long. It was Ed's parents and their son—my best and only friend, whom I thought I had lost forever.

He had changed so much I hardly recognized him. He was tall—a handsome guy with a swagger I had never seen before. He was now a grown man. I gave them all polite hugs, careful not to show my real feelings. My parents were happy to see them, even though they no longer practiced the same faith. After hugs and handshakes all around, the adults decided "us kids" should go on a date! A date? I was seventeen and had never been on a date; I had never been allowed to go on one. The watchful eye of my stepfather saw to that. Dating was just not part of my life. The adults told us he had to take me on a date to get a hamburger. I could have just died, as I was so embarrassed. No one on earth could ever be as embarrassed as a seventeen-year-old girl who had never been on a date being pushed to go out with her best friend from childhood! He did not *ask* me to go. We were *told!* My mom insisted I dress for this hamburger date. She took me into her room and picked a long, silky blue dress with a large white ruffle at the hem. She pinned it in and up so it fit. She even had me apply lipstick, which I had never been allowed to wear. I even had my braids put up, curled around my head in a kind of Heidi fashion. I knew one didn't "dress" to get a hamburger; one just wore slacks or a skirt! (Jeans were not allowed at school and definitely not at church, and I had only work jeans for the farm—nothing I could be seen in public with. Here I was, in a silk fancy dress with my hair making me look like one of the kids from *The Sound of Music*, my braids wrapped over the top of my head, on my first date ever with a grown-up guy, not the kid who ran through the fields with me, to get a stupid hamburger!)Sh---!

At 8:00 p.m. in those days, in the Maine countryside there was not much open. He escorted me to the car as though I was a fine lady. As he opened the door, I could hear the chuckles from the guys gathered on the front porch, with calls of, "Don't run out of gas now!" Ha ha. Dirty minds. I was embarrassed, praying hard that the damn ground would just freakin' *open* already! But I would be *damned* if I would show it! I walked to the car with my head up and a straight back, smiling for them with my first lipstick for them all to see, as if I wore it every day of my life! He put the radio on to strains of Patsy Cline; Peter, Paul, and Mary; and the Browns. We drove up to Belfast, which was about an hour away. We thought surely there was a place to get a hamburger there. Remember, this was the sixties. You couldn't just go get one like you can now. The radio changed my mood as we both sang along with Peter, Paul, and Mary. They sang in my range, and it was great. I knew all the words, and Ed had an amazing voice from all the years of singing in church.

When we got to Belfast, nothing was open. We were starving, but there was nothing to do but start back. Ed saw a light on in a small family restaurant. We pulled up in the driveway, and he got out and went to check. Nope, they were closing.

We sat for a few minutes in embarrassed silence, not saying anything. He gently put his hand on my shoulder and said he had missed me so very much. Looking into my eyes, he said he had written me every day and that when I never responded, he thought I was seeing someone, or that I had tuned into a good church girl and did not care for him any longer. My blood ran cold. I realized with a shock why I was *never* allowed to bring the mail in. Only my stepfather got the mail. The excuse was that because my mother ran a real estate business from the house the mail was important, and we kids would drop it or lose it. They never gave me my mail! I never knew. I started to cry softly. He put his arm around me and moved a bit closer. I slid into his warm arms. Suddenly the love I had for my friend returned. But it was diffcrent—not as it had been when I was a child. The closeness of his body, the warmth of his arms, the soft sent of his cologne, and the tender, sweet kiss on my forehead, left me unhinged and wanting more. I felt my body respond, but I was thinking, *No, we cannot go there*—wherever "there" was. I had no real idea. I was still a virgin. (The dark one had other ways of control for someone of my age.) Yes, I grew up on a farm and knew how things were done, but I had never felt like this—wanting, not daring, not wanting to be bad. I was not a bad girl.

His lips moved over mine. My lips and body responded. His tongue softly explored my mouth. I had no idea. His tongue seemed to reach my toes! His hand slid up my stockings and stopped right at the top, not touching my bare skin. How could I want more and not want more at the same time? His hands held my head.

His lips left mine, and he just held my shaking body. He knew. He said, "No, this is not the time or place. I will never hurt you. Don't worry; I will always love you. When the time is right, I will find you, and we will be together." I looked into his bright, glistening, blue eyes. With a shock, I realized I had found them— the eyes that had been in my dreams all of my life, nearly every night. The eyes—they were here; they had always been here. This was my connection to the stars—our stars.

When we arrived home, I was still shaken. My mother looked me over to see if anything was out of place. The guys poked each other in the ribs, laughing and asking whether we had gotten "lost in the woods." His mom, being upset with their behavior, told them all to stop it. She came over and put her arm around me and asked me whether I had had a good time. I said I had, but I added that I was starving because nothing was open. They had come from Connecticut and had forgotten that Maine, at that time, was still a sleepy place.

Soon they left. It was a long drive to their motel room and then back to Connecticut. We were cool in front of everyone. We said good-bye with well wishes all around. Mother took her dress back, and I went to bed, tiptoeing so as not to wake up one of the babies. I always had at least one of them in my room or in my bed. With my head under my covers and the sheet stuffed in my mouth, I cried myself to sleep.

Thinking about the evening brought back the feelings of the connectedness we'd had years before. Four years seems like an eternity when you are young. I recalled the wonderful flying adventures that we could tell no one about, the things we saw in the night sky that no one would believe, and the eyes. Finally, I knew. I knew why they had always been there. Other lifetimes started coming back to me. I was happy and relaxed and felt loved for the first time in many years.

I left! For the first time since we were separated four years prior, I was able to fly over the rooftop and over the orchard, following the deer and other forest animals. Freedom! I was loved again and knew that no matter what, my heart would always be safe. I could fly, and I did so as often as I could! My friend loved me. I knew in my heart and soul that this was true. I knew somehow life would turn again and someday we would be together. It was the most truth in my world. He would return. Until then, life would go on. I would follow the rules of the house to stay alive. I would do what I had to do until he returned someday. And the dark one would not be able to harm me ever again.

We had giant logs outlining our driveway to separate the driveway from the lawn. The logs were huge. When I had a chance to be alone, I would go out and run back and forth on the top of the logs over and over. Then, if no one was around to bother me, I would find myself over the rooftop. I could fly across the fields and up with the birds and chicken hawks. They never bothered me. It was amazing to feel the strength and moving air of the larger flying birds. I'm sure they could not see me, but maybe they could sense me. I don't know. I could fly with them, and it was wonderful.

If I were called or interrupted in any way, I would find myself running back and forth on the logs. Years later, when I was studying with my friend Bill, a local medicine man, I learned that the rhythm of running, drumming, or my breath, along with the focus of my mind, allowed me to lift from my physical body and "fly." It was only when my concentration was broken by someone calling me or interrupting me that I would return to my body. Anyone in the yard watching me could not tell that I wasn't there. Over the years, I found that many different kinds of rhythms could help me be in a different space.

Little did Ed and I know that by the time life turned on it's axis again, in the late nineties and we reconnected, nearly fifty years would have passed. By then we had both married others, had families, had gotten divorced and remarried, and divorced again. And life amazingly moved on as it wanted to, whether we were paying attention to it or not.

Late Sixties

I married one of our farm hands right out of high school. He was three years ahead of me in school. He came from a large family and knew farming. I didn't see any other way out. So, when he said he thought we should get married, I said yes. The depression I was feeling about my situation went deep. I hadn't had any "seeing dreams" for what seemed like years. I couldn't get a bead on what choices were the best to make. What was I to do about my siblings? Would they be safe if I wasn't there? My mother didn't want me to leave, because I was the babysitter and cook, and I could calm down the dark one when I saw he was drinking too much and had his guns out. But I had no transportation. I did have a small job in Belfast in the "pants factory." I depended on transportation from a neighbor. All money earned went to the house. I lived there, and any of us who were working "out" gave their money to support the house. The older boys were working "out" by that time. After all, our parents said that since they were feeding us, it was only fair for those who were working to support the whole. The house rule was "You work, you pay."

I wanted to go to school. I could hardly attend the school I was in, as I had to keep taking days off to care for the kids. I was so happy on days I could actually go. I didn't know how to go on to school. No one ever told me how to get to college to learn to be a real doctor. I knew education cost money, but I had no idea how to get it. My guidance counselor said I was only going to have babies anyway and didn't see why I would want to go to school. I really thought I could just teach myself to be a midwife. I had delivered babies before (one human, a few goats, and assorted small critters); it wasn't that hard! I figured that was a kind of a doctor, and they really didn't have to do much except clean up the mess. I didn't

60

understand anything about the world. The first time I ever saw a conveyor belt in a store to carry groceries between my basket and the cashier was after I had married. I didn't know what it was or how to put my groceries on it. Before that, I thought conveyors were only used to bring hay from the ground to the top of the barn! A conveyor for groceries—what a phenomenal idea! I knew about plants and herbs and where to put my hands when I saw colors, but I had no idea how the real world worked.

I had been married about six years and had two kids and was living on a small dirt farm in Maine. My husband mostly worked the farm in season, with no income till the crops came in in the fall. He worked in the local chicken plant in winter. I babysat in my home for the neighbors to make a bit extra. He would become furious when anything didn't go his way. As long as I didn't talk back and had supper ready and on time, the kids and I were pretty much okay. However, he refused to take me to the doctor once when I had a bad allergy attack. I drove myself after I called the doctor in town, and he was waiting for me in the parking lot with a needle in his hand! He saved my life!

Even though the boys' father had wanted at least a dozen kids (he was the youngest of twenty-four siblings from the same parents, all single births), he didn't want his own around underfoot. I didn't have a choice. I didn't have a car so couldn't leave on my own. Even though I was living in the country, life was not so good. We drank water from an open hand-dug well. In the summer, it wasn't too bad. We put our milk down the well to keep it cold. In the winter, we melted snow for cooking and washing and had no heat most of the time. But we had two large greenhouses and had a truck garden in season.

A Day of Hope and Distress

One day an old blue car rolled into the driveway. I watched, thinking it was one of the local farmers there to see my husband. I looked again and was shocked when the driver walked up to the door. I couldn't believe my eyes. It was my friend Harvey, who now was called Ed. My heart jumped into my mouth! I couldn't speak and was embarrassed as I tried not to stammer! I had my grubby farm clothes on and knew I looked a fright! I just stared at him when he asked whether he could come in. Red-faced and stammering like an idiot, I waved for him to come in, and he did. Suddenly I was a stammering sixteen-year-old again. We talked for hours, the kids clambering around him as if they had known him for years. We talked about memories and what our lives were like now, and we just talked excitedly, seemingly for hours.

Eventually he got ready to go. I knew it was coming, but my heart still sank. I hated the idea of his going, but what could I do? He asked me whether I wanted to pack up the kids and come with him. I firmly said no. I was married, and no matter what, the answer was no. We hugged with tears in our eyes. I knew I would never see him again. As he dejectedly walked down the driveway, I wondered whether I might have lost my chance to make a new life. But I had given my oath; I was married. Unbeknownst to me, he was there because he'd had a dream that my kids and I were in a bad situation. He had searched everywhere, going through old phone numbers and addresses, until he found me, but he never said a word about what he knew. He left with tears gleaming as they ran down his face, never having a clue that his life was about to change more than he could ever guess. Within six months, he was invited to go on a yearlong vacation at the expense of the state. Not a fun time was had by all.

Life on Our Dirt Farm

The boy's dad had learned to farm in a certain way. Everything was done the hard way. Having come from a large family as well, I didn't know the difference. Every kid had his chores, such as shelling peas without eating them at age three. Their father, being the youngest of twenty-four, had had many teachers. He had learned that kids were for work. One needed them to run the farm. That's why one had them. Not that there was much of a choice back then in the far country; people got what God gave them. His mom had her first child at fourteen and her last at thirty-eight.

In a few more years, we had three 100'×40' Quonset hut–type greenhouses. These provided more than enough work for all of us. The boys learned how to plant, raise, and sell. Eventually we became a seed company at about the same time Johnny's Selected Seeds came into the New England market. They were our direct competitor. We couldn't beat 'em with our old-fashioned style of farming. Even in the early days, with one kid in a playpen under the tree and one tied to my hip on the John Deere with a double-blade plow and a four-blade disk harrow, we just couldn't prep the fields in time or plant in time to grow a good harvest. Then if it rained too much or not enough, we were doomed from the beginning. I just never saw it. For years I figured that if I could work harder we would make it. But working the land by hand with a couple of broken down pieces of equipment could not hold water to the larger farms with real up to date equipment. ...

I was strict with my kids because that was all I knew, but we also had fun. Living deep in the country, there was time to do other things when we weren't planting or harvesting. I taught them how to cook. They were both accomplished bread makers by age twelve. They took drum and saxophone lessons for as long as I could afford to pay for them. I had to argue with their dad to let them learn or to even go to school. He believed that school was useless, and they were needed on the farm. At eight and nine, the boys helped their dad spread chicken manure with the spreader, sometimes driving the tractor. They were also responsible for our motley crew of chickens and a guinea pig.

I taught them what little I knew about the stars, earth, science, constellations, herbs, country medicine, and wild life. In my spare time, I wrote wannabe music and poetry and taught the boys how to make treasure mapsalways believing they could come true.

1980s

My husband and I divorced after twelve years of marriage. There had been infidelities on his part, and I could no longer honor my oath. The boys and I moved into an old New England home in a larger town—a thirteen-room house in the middle of a four-hundred-acre apple orchard. We had heat, water, a cellar, plenty of room to run and play, and extra rooms to lease in our wonderful rented home. I was shocked out of my wits when I walked through the entry room into the kitchen for the first time. The kitchen was a bright yellow, and the walls were a white-and-yellow plaid. It had a silver dishwasher and white stove and wonderful full windows looking out into the amazing orchard. I had seen this *all* before years prior, when I was teaching the boys to make treasure maps just to keep them occupied on dreary winter days. This kitchen was what I had seen, but in reality! It exactly matched a picture I had cut out and pasted on a piece of cardboard! I was standing right in the middle of *my* kitchen! We lived in this amazing orchard home for nearly ten years. I went on to start a business called Healing Focus, which offered classes, massage therapy, and energy work. I was one of the first licensed massage therapists in the state of Maine at that time. I started writing instead of just stuffing words like sausages into my brain! I did a series on our local public TV station on stress, family massage, and holistic health, and I also did several radios shows. I created a massage video, two cassette tapes, and a CD on relaxation and meditation. Life was moving in directions I had never known were possible. Ideas I thought were only silly imaginings became real life.

Nixon 1972

I remember watching President Nixon on the Great Wall of China through a grainy black-and-white TV when I was a young woman. It was amazing! That news program opened the world, or at least my world, to other possibilities and ways of thinking. I realized for the first time that many things in the world happened at the same time in different places. I had never thought like that before, but I'd had had little access to the outside world up until that time. I decided then and there that I wanted to go to China and walk, see, touch, and feel the Great Wall! I could feel the pull inside my mind and heart. I could *feel* the excitement of going. Then I promptly forgot about that idea and went about my chores. What was the point? I had no education, certainly not enough money to figure out how to get there, and two young boys running around that I was responsible for. At least in my conscious mind, I forgot about it. Who knows what lurks in the far depths of that gray softness or what ancient thoughts float to the top? What wiggles around unbeknownst to us into the correct configuration to bring our pictures and beliefs about in real life? Nearly seventeen years later, in 1989, I was walking on the Great Wall!

I never thought of how or why I would go. I never saw myself getting on a plane or learning Chinese. I just saw myself there. I organized nothing, but life organized things.

I learned many possibilities of healing during the short time I was there. China opened the door for me to many learnings and insights that came into my life as the years went by. Over time, I learned how to use various popular methods of feeling, seeing, and moving energy. Imagery was the first. I would "think" or "see" someone well while I put my hands on him or her. My hands got hot, and the person got better.

Sometimes I could "vision" the situation and use my mind vision to help. A friend called from out of state. Her mom was having a serious liver problem. The doctors were not as successful in correcting the situation as they had expected. I worked on her from a distance. It seemed I was not getting anywhere, so I changed tactics. I asked myself, "How else can dark spots be removed?" The idea came to me to "see" the liver and use a mental pencil eraser to remove them. The idea came to me to think outside the box regarding different ways to use my mind energy, so I did. I got a picture of a liver from an anatomy book so I could "vision" it correctly. I "saw" the liver with dark spots, and in my mind, I erased the spots with a pencil eraser. I kept at it for a few hours until I could no longer see the spots in my mind. Three days later, the daughter called and said the doctors were so surprised that her mom's tests had come back clear. Now, would this have happened anyway? Who knows? I was as shocked as anyone. Slowley, I learned the connection between mind, belief and "energy". Then I learned about therapeutic touch. I was in nursing school. It was the rage, and most RNs in hospitals were trained in it. Then came Reiki, then Karuana Reiki, and then Quantum Touch and other forms of energy work, or light work. The more structured energy work methods helped me put proper boundaries around the work I was doing. I could see the "edges" more clearly. I practiced many of these methods. Little by little, I was exposed to other teachings about using mind and emotional energy to make a difference in my life as well as in others' lives. The teachers and guides I have been blessed to have throughout my life have been amazing. They put lots of energy into teaching a stubborn young woman with an attitude that there was more—so very much more. They never gave up on me. For that I am grateful. They and the lessons I learned proved to me that life is multidimensional and connects with us and everything, everywhere, in many ways. This learning is available to everyone who seeks that path. Because Ed had much deeper learning and understanding than I had because of his relationship with shamans and the lessons they taught, years later when life opened that door again, I was able to learn from him as well, and we worked together in tandem. However, I could never get into the depths inside that he could reach. He never spoke about his work and never refused any request. His energy was always freely given to anyone who would ask. As I learned about treasure maps and vision boards, I started teaching workshops and classes to show people, especially women, how, by creating storyboards, they could help direct the pathways of their lives. The storyboards were like the storyboards film crews follow when filming a movie.

As time went on, I found other materials to learn from, and I discovered that the storyboard was not just about envisioning something and trusting it would come true. There was a hidden component in making one's pictures a reality. That component was the feeling of the emotional energy of the essence of the board being created. That was the moving point that could turn it into a reality. I discovered that when one feels the emotion of the essence of the board being created, life can and will make it so. This requires believing in what one is feeling, not just cutting out a picture. It does not specifically require working toward the creation one is pasting on one's board, but projecting the feeling forward each time one envisions it, allowing oneself to *feel* the emotion as one brings one's vision into one's real life.

. The red car, mountains, piano, and motorcycle in my most recent board did not mean I wanted a new red car or any of those things. I chose those pictures because they made me feel good. I wanted to create a situation in my life of feeling good and healthy and having the means I needed. The combination of pictures I chose gave me the feeling of moving forward and being supported. (However, if you offered me a red car, I wouldn't turn you down!) I finally figured out that my board meant abundance and joy. That was the emotion that came up each time I looked at it. That was the point that I wasn't teaching at the time, because I didn't realize it. That was the connection between Nixon and my going to China. I didn't organize it; life did!

Until about a month before I went, I had no idea at all that I was going. I felt a strong emotion about a news program as a young woman. Unbeknownst to me, that sight changed my life. The emotion made an unknown mark on me, and when the time was right, life intervened and created just what I needed to go and to study in China!

I call this "imprinting." This is similar to the way a baby chick or other baby animal will imprint on one of the first things it sees and will follow that thing as if that thing is its mother. When you are emotionally moved by something either good or bad, that thing tends to constantly come up in your life. But you may not remember a thing about it in your subconscious life. Even the belief system you grew up with will have a subconscious impact on your life, though you may never realize it. It took me most of my life to figure that out. Even though others had figured it out and were teaching it. I just didn't get the connection for years. This is not a scientific explanation. Well, imprinting is a real phenomenon. There are scientific explanations about energy and all of its aspects as we are trying to communicate through our amazing adventures. This is our version of some aspects of energy and how we can use it. You can find the scientific facts behind this life phenomena if you want to look them up through the science of physics and quantum theory. It may sound as if it's hard to understand, but put very simply, physics is the study of how and why things move. Quanta are tiny, invisible to the eye, moving parts that seem to have intelligence. The word "theory" is just a way of saying someone thought of this idea. See? A theory is a person's reasoning for why something we *think* works in a given way works in that way So, extremely simply put, Physics is just studying the how and why of energetic parts that move and may have some form of consciousness! I know a real scientist would see this description as silliness, but sometimes silliness makes us chuckle, and that is not all bad!

When I cut out magazine pictures of a beautiful yellow kitchen, we were living with no running water and no heat. It was winter. We were melting snow for drinking and cooking. The boys and I were all huddled together in my bed to keep warm. I had them cut pictures out of magazines to give them something to do. When I saw the picture of that kitchen, I just had to have it! I remember grinning from ear to ear. *Someday I will have that kitchen!* I thought, smiling. At that moment, that amazing yellow kitchen was so beautiful, and I so wanted it! It wasn't about the kitchen itself; it was about the fact that I knew that if I could have that kitchen, I would also have room, heat, and water. The important part was the essence of what that kitchen represented. I have learned a truth about the phrase "You get what you ask for." You may not always choose the time or place, but you will always get what you ask for. I *knew* it. I had heard those words many times and was taught this belief by many master teachers, but I still didn't get it! So be mindful, as thoughts are things—or will be things. Choose only the best ones. We often think only in linear ways because we are human and were taught that way of thinking and seeing, but all energy is multidimensional. Even us. We just have never been taught the possibilities!

I returned from China, and life was going well. Ed was living and working in Florida, going through his own life situations. We had talked to each other by phone only once a year or so up to that point. I was driving down Main Street in Lewiston, Maine, and a car bumped into the back of me. No harm was done; it just caused a jolt. I checked for damage, and there was little. Everyone was okay, so I headed home. I didn't have a cell phone in those days, and when I got into the house, my phone was ringing. It was Ed! He breathlessly asked me whether I was okay and whether I was hurt. I asked him what he was talking about. He said, "You just had a car accident, didn't you?" I explained that I'd had a fender bender and no one was hurt. I was shocked by his call, although I should not have been. He had picked up on the accident while he was in the middle of something else. He felt I had had an accident, but he had no idea how bad it might have been. He was calling to make sure I was okay. This kind of seeing is called clairvoyance, or clear vision. He was also a "sensitive," meaning he often felt things before he saw them. I am a sensitive as well. If he had been fully focused on what he had seen or felt, he would have been able to decipher just what had happened and would have known that no one had been hurt. Sometimes when you let your emotions get involved, you do not get a clear reading of what you may be seeing or feeling.

Learning in the Early Years

I learned something during those years. Life is really lived backwards. Most of us don't realize this until we are nearly finished with it. Through introspection and the bright flashes of dreams here and there, I could still weave pictures together. I figured out that as we live, we learn how to treat others. What we have been taught, and the experiences we live as we grow up are all part of our day-to-day learning. Until it's our turn, we have no idea what we've learned. Sometimes dawn comes late over Marble Head! It took me years to learn or to accept that someone or something was trying to teach me or show me something. I just stomped my foot and said, "No! I will do it by myself, my way!" It took what seems like eons and a near death (mine) to finally get it! Yes, I had gotten the message, but I would *not* listen! After all, I was a grown-up now and could figure it out by myself! So there!

Over the years, I had forgotten many of the early dreams and messages that told me about my life and helped me understand decisions. It was easier to cut my insights off than deal with the ridicule and fear that people were directing at me. Those messages were gone with the wind. They were too painful to stay with openly. I left what I knew was the truth in my heart. Life was hard. Life was frustrating. I was ready to just give up. I felt I could no longer stand this knowing, not knowing, or doing, as well as the miserableness of not having anyone to share these ideas with. I just felt more depressed and crazier. What can you do when you have been taught that your beautiful, loving gifts are really evil?

When I returned from China, I met a man who seemed to be interesting and interested in my travels and my work. There was something wrong, but I couldn't put my finger on it. After a year, we decided to marry. My gut did not like the idea; it felt like a rock whenever I thought about it. At that point, I had been single for fourteen years. My kids were grown and gone. I figured it was time to make changes. I started having dark dreams again, but I brushed them away. After all, I wasn't a kid any more. I could take care of myself. My friends came to me and said this was not a good decision. The day we signed the marriage papers, I had to leave the courthouse to throw up. Part of me knew that this was not a good situation and that I should not continue. Did I listen? No! I was still the willful brat! I nearly lost my life by not listening.

Eight years later, the phone rang. It was Ed. I was shocked. I never expected to hear from him. He had his own life going on. And now I was married, again. He said he'd had been having dreams that someone was trying to harm me. Everything he told me he had dreamt about was true! I was shocked. I wanted to believe that the things that were happening—or that I thought were happening—were all in my mind. Eventually I was able to divorce my husband. It was a frightening time. This person was not stable. My life was truly in danger.

Around 2000, Ed and I married. We were reunited after nearly fifty years.

Our Insight About Vibrations and Other Sacred Connections

We are not physicists. We are two people who had natural experiences that most others thought were odd or bad. We didn't believe that we were bad, or odd. We knew we were different but puzzled about all that we were experiencing. We don't know the ins and outs of the quantum world, but we are sensible. We understood many scientific things because when seemingly impossible things happened to us over time, we researched medicine, science, and religions around the world, as best we could. We worked at putting two and two together. *We hope you will take these words in a way that fit for you.* Our Creator put these things together in ways we will never understand. We know that everything is connected and sacred. We were given free will out of love and to enable us to make a difference *if we choose to do so*, which we all can. Since Ed and I are not traditionally educated in the sciences, we have tried to break down the science as we understand it into the smallest and easiest to understand ideas possible. Real scientists will laugh their heads off. But we thought that if we could just paint a picture of how things may connect, it would be easier for nonscientific people to grasp all of the lines of connected pathways.

Plants, animals, people, rocks, and dirt—everything past, present, and future—everything is connected. This includes our thoughts, our energy, our souls, the good, the bad, and the ugly. Everything. If we were all taught this truth from birth, think of what kind of different world we would have! We do know that over centuries many things have been hidden because of the belief systems of various rulers and governments, political differences, language differences, and differences in spiritual belief systems around the world. Some of our scriptures have been changed from their original wordings for many reasons over the centuries. That makes it more difficult for us to understand meanings and ideas that may have been changed over time. Wrong understanding may have come about often as a result of not fully understanding another's language or customs. We believe that our Creator, whoever or whatever that may be, knows us. This unimaginable power is part of who we are. I think we have a very powerful and sensible Creator ... Well, unless you look at the duck-billed platypus! A duck's bill, a mammal's fur, webbed feet, lays eggs like a bird—and doesn't even have feathers! Interesting combo! But then I guess that shows a sense of humor, which is not a bad thing. Our learning on this earth may be difficult at times; at least our Creator had the good sense to give us something to laugh about!

Yes, I know that when someone says we are all connected, many roll their eyes and say, "Yep! More 'out there stuff!" But just think about it. In today's world, we understand the words "microbe," "cell," "molecule," "atom," "electron," "photon," and more to refer to tiny things unseen by the naked eye—things that are part of our bodies and our world. We all know that these are small particles that are part of us, but we rarely put that knowledge into a true understanding. Ed and I are endeavoring to share what we have learned about vibrations in simple understandable ways, as well as some of the other amazing things we have learned over all our years together and apart.

Everything on Earth, off Earth, and in all of the possible universes—ours and others—is made of moving parts. As the parts move, they create vibrations. These vibrations make sounds. Sounds and their vibrations, as well as the light they create, travel and impact everything they touch or even move near. Scripture tells us that in the beginning God said, "Let There Be Light!"(Genesis 1:3) God's voice, like ours, has moving parts, as we do. Perhaps I should say we have moving parts as *he* does. God spoke with intent. Intent is what helps us negotiate our world and lets our creative selves create. All of creation works together with intent. Intent is the power we have to move and change from our inside out.

Our scriptures tell us in many places that our Creator is within. Our Creator is not some old guy sitting on a throne with a stick, ready to nail us if we are not good. We believe that God is everywhere, including inside us. He always was, always is, and always will be. The love our Creator has for us is forever and unbounded. We and our earth will never be destroyed by the hand of our Creator. We have free will to follow the rules or not. We decide and sow as we reap. We have the free will to destroy our earth if we so choose. The mess our world is in at this time is not because God is punishing us because we disobeyed. It is because we have chosen this path through our actions. Remember the Newtonian physics we learned in school? "To every action there is an equal and opposite reaction." We are causing this reaction, and we can choose to fix it.

In some long-past cultures, people made mandalas—drawn symbols, usually created to be round. (The creation of the universe is always seen as round, with no sharp corners, by those considered "healers and teachers" of their time and culture.)) They were made with interpreted ideas and visions of symbols, angles and colors that were seen and felt from the vibrations that people of that time could see and hear. They understood that we were all connected—people, plants, animals, water, rocks, earth, and planets. They knew the entire universe was made up of vibrations and sound frequencies given to us by our Creator.

It was their intent to teach others—perhaps those not of their current time—how vibrations were made, identified, and used, and how those vibrations were part of their worship, their healing, or their living their day-to-day lives to connect with the Creator. Indigenous people knew this truth.

Each "picture" or color representing the "look and feel" of sound was created as part of the understanding of the universe. Mandalas also show us what certain sounds "looked" like. In our culture today, a picture of a musical note does the same thing. A line of notes is a line of sounds depicting the order in which the notes should be sounded. So, we can understand the language of music, or sound vibration. A learned person can understand what each musical note means and what it should sound like. If we do not pass this information on, a thousand years from now people will see these funny-looking symbols sitting on straight lines and wonder what they were. They may not even have a clue what they were or how to use them. Someday when they find out that "we ancients" left this information for them, they may struggle to find a clue and figure out what it all means, just as we do when researching our own pasts.

A musical note symbol tells us what the sound is like or what its vibration level is. Other symbols on a page of music offer information about various aspects of how a note or series of notes are to be performed. These symbols help people communicate through sound. This lets the musician understand the music sound system, or what the vibrations of sound mean, regardless of what language he or she speaks. People can learn to read and sound notes no matter what language they speak. Music has always been considered a universal language. In past times, people used pictures in the same way to show what a vibration would sound like. They had no way of sharing their healing sounds except through pictures when people were long distances apart. These "sound pictures" were also used as a kind of time capsule of the day. People knew that as time went on and cultures changed, their insight may be lost over time. They believed that mandalas would secure the information so that people in other generations would not lose the knowledge of how to communicate with the universe or God. They left these pictures in the hope that others would understand them and would keep the vibrations and knowledge of the universe alive, whether they be tones from the earth or sounds from the voices of humans. Even the magnetic field around the earth has its own sound, as do all of the suns and planets. We have lost much knowledge over the many centuries and through various cultural changes. Now we are trying to relearn the knowledge of these pictures and their correlating sounds as we relearn what they could have meant. Mandalas and musical notes are both created by mathematical equations. Everything in the universe is based on math.

It is believed by some that disruptions in our vibrations cause our bodies and minds to become ill. Ed and I believe that one day vibrational medicine will be more understood and become part of our everyday lives. Those of us who use the laying on of hands or prayer energy by any name are using vibrations to help body, mind, and heart heal.

Each vibration has its own frequency. Frequency is a way to describe vibration. Everything vibrates—even things we think are not alive. Rocks, for example, don't move on their own, but their energy within vibrates. The vibrations are very slow, but the frequencies can be measured. A quartz crystal and an opal both vibrate, but they vibrate at different frequencies. Many natural stones and crystals have vibrations that match the vibrations of different parts of our bodies. That is the reason some people feel more well or comfortable if they pick a stone or crystal that vibrates at the same frequency that is needed to bring them back to a state of calmness or to their healthiest selves.

Each vibration has a frequency that can be measured. For example, the A on the middle of a keyboard vibrates at 440 Hz. That means it is vibrating 440 times a second. A rose has the highest vibration of any plant, at 320 Hz, and being near them or even thinking of them firmly in your mind will bring your own vibrations up. (This is one of the reasons we all feel so good when we are around or smell roses. It's a living plant sending us vibrations of love! [The human heart, on its own, has a vibratory rate of about 0.1 Hz.] Roses, their oil, and even pictures of roses can increase the feeling of love. Feelings are movement, and they have a vibratory energy that can leave our bodies and affect others.) These vibrations are not about blood pressure; they relate to the vibrational relationships to each cell from the nearness or the thought vibration around it. Our hearts correlate their vibrations (not heartbeats) to the vibrational frequency of the rose. That is why rose oil is so extremely expensive—approximately $400 per ounce for the real stuff! I have a very tiny amount that I use sparingly. Sometimes I just sniff the aroma and send it mentally to one who has asked for help. It is one of the most potent energy-healing plants there is. If we can learn to increase our vibrations, our bodies will start to absorb the vibrations and start to heal at all levels. Roses are the traditional gift of love. This makes me think about the correlation. How did anyone figure that one out? Mmmmm ...

Pythagoras, in the sixth century, was a philosopher who was also credited with being the father of geometry, as well as the father of Western music theory. He put these two insights together and realized that letters and numbers have frequencies that work together in supporting each other's reality. The vibrations of music (or sound), math, and letters make up the frequencies that allow us to have life and connections with everything.

I use tuning forks in my work when I'm balancing someone's energy. I find that this sacred ratio of 2:3 has an ability to stop migraine headaches almost immediately. The forks that I use are known as Pythagorean tuning forks. (2:3 represents Pi. pi is the creation-wide mathematical calculation that flows through everything in the universe, from snail shells to our own DNA. The decimal representation of pi [3.14159 …] goes on for infinity and is found throughout our entire universe.) If you have an interest, I have added to the back of the book the contact information of my source for tuning forks. I have no relationship to the company, and this is not an ad. I'm just happy to help you find what you may be looking for.

Lower tones have slower frequencies than higher ones. Humans can hear sounds as low as 16 Hz and as high as 16,000 Hz. Just because we cannot hear a sound doesn't mean it does not exist. Small children can hear sounds around 20,000 Hz. A possible reason a child may be fussy or not sleeping well is that the child may be hearing sounds or feeling vibrations that we as adults cannot detect. The sounds a child hears may be disturbing to them. Did you know dolphins and whales can send and receive sounds of 180,000 Hz? That is well beyond what human ears can hear!

There is a science called cymatics. This science shows the interplay of vibration and form, energy and matter. It also seeks to explain the interplay between water and sound. Amazingly, when vibration is added to water, the patterns that appear are always the same, depending on which frequency is being used. The water makes patterns at certain frequencies that are the exact replicas of ancient mandalas! How did people of those times figure this out and understand what they were seeing or how to use the knowledge? Go figure! This is so astounding! The information is amazing and really makes you think about the science behind everyday insights into our world. Understanding this knowledge can open so many new doors to our understanding of ourselves, our universe, and our connections to everything. You will be continuously amazed as you come to this understanding step by step.

If you are interested in sounds and how sound waves and vibrations affect our lives and thoughts, you might enjoy *Dancing Wu Li Masters* by Gary Zukav. This is an easily comprehensible work about quantum physics and quantum mechanics and how these invisible bits of energy affect our lives and our thinking.

Our Intro to Psychic Ability or What Does Spirit Have to Do With It?

Psychic ability has always been a part of our family history. Since both Ed and I have been blessed with some of these gifts, we thought it was important for us to bring people to an understanding (ours anyway) of why we believe we have these gifts and how we believe they work, as well as the terms for the ways we might receive this information. Overall, that's what this book is about. We tried to bring in basic and simplified scientific understanding, as well as the simple idea of quanta. We want to help people understand what is happening to them and not be fearful or think they are crazy.

My grandfather on my mother's side was a family physician and a hands-on healer, as stated earlier. He was also clairvoyant. ("Clairvoyant" refers to a person who has "clear vision." Like when you see "colors" around a person, of perhaps see a glimps of a loved one who has passed on "Clairaudient" refers to a person who has "clear hearing"—such as when one hears one's mom's voice and she has been gone for some years, but one recognizes her voice and pays attention!) My mother's father would know if my mother misbehaved at school, and he would be ready to scold her when she got home. She couldn't do anything without her father knowing! My mother and her sister also had some of these gifts. My aunt saw many of my grandfather's patients recover from serious illness in minutes right under his hands. She insisted she saw him bring a woman back from death after she had been pronounced dead and covered. Grandfather came in about a half hour later and brought her back enough to retrieve an important piece of family information the husband had been begging to find out while she was passing. When grandfather got the information, he laid her back down and let her go. My aunt swears this is true. During the war, the family kept hidden to stay alive. At one point near the end of the war, my grandfather was captured, nailed to a tree, and left to die because he would not work with the Nazis. He was rescued by American soldiers. During the war, my mother was involved in working with the Nazis to try to see enemy bases through clairvoyance—or remote viewing, as it started to be called. ("Remote viewing" did not sound as spooky as "clairvoyance!") The viewers also tried to contact spirits or aliens through psychic powers. In retrospect, I think that was the reason she was so terrified when she realized I had some of these gifts too. I never knew, until I met Ed at about ten years old, that other people had these abilities as well.

Ed has and had many more abilities then I have. He was also taught by several native tribes their medicine ways and how to use them. His learning focused on projection, or travel and protection. Travel was what he did when he went out of his body. He learned how to do it at will, as well as how to project an idea or physical sensation to another, such as the scent of oranges or a vision of the sea. He had been given power animals, or spirit animals, by his teachers. He was able to send them to someone, and that person could actually see them. They felt these animals would help them stay safe. I was in danger once, years before we were back together in real life again. I sat in shock, watching the animals come out of the fireplace and sit next to me. As I relaxed, they faded away, as I no longer needed their support. I was calm, and the danger was gone. I reached out to him and asked him what he had been doing that evening. Without a hint, he told me what he had sent and why. He described it exactly as it had unfolded in front of the fire.

Ed was raised in a religious community and was beaten badly by his father if he "consorted with the devil," which included anything out of the norm—even a hunch out of the blue! They believed the demons were trying to get him. Our family worshiped in the same way as well, for a few years. The latent fear of punishment stayed with him internally for years. I often wondered whether, had he gotten through the fear, he would have developed an even better understanding of his energy and ability.

Thoughts about Some of Our Teachings and Learnings

Ed

I have had teachers who could teach only one thing. It was what they had to contribute to the whole. Not all teachers teach all things. If your gift is to teach humor and mine is to teach survival and someone else teaches humility, then the pupil of these three teachers will become more rounded by these many chisels. Don't withhold your light from the world because of a perceived lack of brightness. Enough small lights together will soon outshine even the sun. The easiest and most trapping (I use "trapping" because the ego will want to get involved, and then you will be working only with an aggrandizement of self) part is getting the subconscious or lower self, not to mean lesser or bad, under control. This is done through thought and imagination or visualization. this is carried out by the part of the mind that can sense radiations from things or people and has the ability to fasten to a person (an invisible thread for types of healing or control, depending on the intended use). That part of us is also called the Innate. It is always listening and ready to follow our directions, although most of us are never taught about this. The ego plays a big part at this level for many. Some so-called teachers are stuck in this space, teaching what they themselves mistakenly call the truth. Many new students put enormous emphasis on telepathic ability. Often, they lose sight of the truth and do not even realize there is more. Because a novice can use this new knowledge for good or evil, this adventure can be very heady.

Ritual and ceremony have their places in worship (giving thanks and celebrating joy), and for beginners, these things help calm the mind and allow students to get into another space, making their gifts easier to access.

To move forward, it is best to move and train with care, to control the lower self, and to integrate the middle and higher selves. These three parts, the Trinity, may be called by other names, depending on which system the teaching comes from.

Sonja

I believe one of the best ways to study the combination of lower, middle, and higher self and understand the relationship to worship and God and get a better understanding and working relationship with them is to research the writing of Max Freedom Long, beginning with *Growing into Light*. He is a researcher of the Huna belief system (Hawaii). We have all heard the word "kahuna." It refers to the head spiritual teacher of the Huna belief system. The information Long presents goes back to the religious writings of the Jews and early Christians but can be understood only when the symbolic meanings of the words are learned. The Gnostic writings of the same general place and period are also of great value. The writings of the early Greek initiates and of Jews who were also versed in the Greek version of the "Secret" gave confirmation of these things learned elsewhere. In India, concealed writings were preserved in a garbled form to keep the masses from having access to them. This information is serious and real. They did not want regular, run-of-the-mill people having access because of the damage that could be done if people used it wrongly for personal gain. The various beliefs and practices, especially the latter, gave conclusive information relating to which version of Huna was once practices in that part of the world by Hindu initiates.

We have striven to introduce these things by giving simple information based on science. We understand that if you are serious, you want to find where you can get more. We did.

Below are simple and, we hope, understandable practices and information that will help you on your path without fear. The Max Freedom Long work will give you a better spiritual understanding of how energy and thought with intention are connected in all of us. It's there all the time for our using, but we must learn how to use it.

If you are a Star Wars fan, you might enjoy reviewing the movies again after all these years. Be mindful of the conversations about energy, force, and mind control. You will see that the movies were not far off the mark of reality. They not only taught possibilities but also opened a door for wider thinking, showing us that we all have free will to choose which side we travel on.

We have tried to keep the information simple and easy to understand. It is real. We try to share the simple beginning parts that most people can master if they have the intention. Ability can be developed. But please don't think this is just fun and games. As you come to understand the depth of these gifts, you will be astounded. People who bring light and offer love freely benefit the whole planet, and even the universe and beyond, because all is connected.

People who are self-serving can cause harm to others. It's their choice. We all have free will. That is the reason for dark tales and stories about the dark side. They are real. But they are not due to some evil thing trying to turn us from God. They are due to our own lack of caring or concern for others, as well as greed and a lack of understanding of how we are all connected and why, or what the result is meant to be if we choose. There was a time in our far past that our ancestors lived in peace and abundance with free will for hundreds or even thousands of years. (Archaeologists have proven this. One of the things that lead to this conclusion is that for long periods of history, there are no tools of war to be found anywhere in any campsite or village.) Some chose the darkness, and when they did, it totally changed the world in that space and time. We live with this mix today, but it is changing, and the light is returning around the world. As the current rot breaks through to the light, all darkness will be seen and change. This will still take some time. Light is more powerful than darkness. As we think, so shall it be. Thinking and feeling are parts of our vibration field all over this planet. We didn't get into this mess in a day or two, but it is changing, and there will be world peace on Earth, in time. So, wherever one's head is, meaning one's consciousness, is what one will offer to the world. Remember: energy is! Energy has no feelings of right or wrong. We do! We direct the energy! The energy does what we consciously or subconsciously direct it to do. The energy can light our house or burn it down. It's energy; it doesn't care. It will follow the path of least resistance and the directions we give it.

How It's Done:
Your One-of-a-Kind Guide

These are our experiences—what we have learned and what we teach. Everyone is different and holds a different belief system. These are the suppositions we have gathered during our lifetime. The insights below are presented in a Q and A format. This is how we answered the questions our students asked us over the years.

~~~~~~~~~~~~~~~

Flying

Q. How can real people get out of their bodies and fly? How do I know this is not a bunch of rubbish?

A. Well, we can only draw from science and our own personal experience to explain possibilities. There is research you can do. There are religious documents that share past stories about monks, priests, and nuns who were seen by others to fly. Eventually they were made saints. I wasn't there, so I don't know for sure.

As a child, the first time I flew in the daytime was an accident. I was around four or five and was playing alone in the backyard. I was just running and trying to jump as high as I could. Suddenly, I was over the housetops, and I could see TV antennas, chimneys, and tools left by repair people on all the roofs around. And I saw many things that I could not see from the backyard three stories below. I was shocked and fell to the ground and tried and tried to do it again, but I could not until years later. Then I learned to fly at will, especially at night. Then I could leave and others who saw me would think I was just asleep.

We are energy. We can and do exist without our bodies in a quantum world. Some call this world heaven or the spirit world. When the time comes to "graduate" from this school of Earth, we leave. Our bodies, the houses we have lived in since before we were born, stay here. We fly! We are free, and we leave without the heaviness of our bodies and our restrictive Earth thinking. Regardless of what we each believe, most of us can agree that we believe we were made and put here out of love by our Creator— or whichever words you use to name that force.

Our astral, or energy, bodies, are made up of sound and light vibrations that extend outside of our physical bodies. When people say they can see or feel energy around another, it's the astral body they are picking up on. (Yep, we can see others sparkle!) They call what is being seen or felt an aura or an energy field. You can find other information on colors and vibration frequencies in other articles online or in books.

Human consciousness seems to be able to move from our physical bodies into our energy bodies during sleep, usually staying about a foot or so above our physical bodies. If you have ever slept like a rock and woken up feeling fantastic, it could be that you left your body so it could heal, and when you came back, you just felt great! You may have been out and about in your energy body and just didn't remember it. (Some of us cannot remember these episodes without training to remember, because the memory may disrupt our physical and emotional lives.) Some of us just can't chew gum and walk at the same time. I'm one; I don't always remember my dreams. I have to make an effort to remember them now. (I think this is also called having a full plate!) But you felt wonderful, as though you just had great, rock-solid sleep! If we remembered every time we left, it would cause problems, because it is not a way most people think. (Or if they do, they keep it to themselves, not wanting to be labeled as nut cases or worse.) Because of the stigma, many won't even admit it to themselves. We have never been taught that we are all multidimensional beings. If we allowed ourselves to believe that, how could we fit into our society, when most don't? Many "normal" people have many extraordinary experiences that are not talked about in "ordinary society."

We were about ten to eleven when we met. Ed secretly told me he could fly. I told him I could too sometimes. We started to fly together at night to amazing and beautiful places.

Since those early days, we learned everything we could about consciousness, healing energy, and energy bodies. We have some understanding of the connection between our lives and the quantum world. We are not scientists, physicists, or mathematicians. I can't even do basic arithmetic unless I take my shoes off! I found that in basic format and in simple ways, it's easy to wrap your head around the quantum world, as long as we don't take simple insights and try to make them absolute! Just envision billions of invisible bits of light flying, almost instantly going beyond supersonic speed, running everything in all the universes! Simple, huh? When we consciously choose to voluntarily leave our bodies for someplace else, its called astral projection. It is not a dream state. You are really where you think you are, without your physical body. Many believe that we are connected to our bodies with silver cords that will release only when we leave our bodies in what we call death.

People who are considered spiritual are often said to leave their bodies. Some examples are Jesus Christ, the disciples, yogis, and shamans. They understood and followed through. There are many others who know how to go into deep meditation. They are consciously choosing to quiet their minds, and they breathe in constructive, rhythmic ways and let their breath guide them out and back. They remember everything and can direct themselves and know where they want to go. They learned how to take action with their minds, as did the masters and gurus of old. Even the healers and shamans of our times have mastered this system. We can as well. It takes stillness and trust. I hope this has given you some of the answers you seek. There is a great deal of information out there. Start researching if you are interested in learning. It is in the quiet that we find peace.

As a simple exercise to help be calm and still, set a timer for ten minutes. Put it under a pillow or in another room so you can hear it but it won't startle you. Lie or sit in a comfortable space, close your eyes, and put your hands over your heart. Breathe out slowly for a count of five, pause for five, and then breathe in for five. Do this slowly until your timer goes off. Breathing at this rate causes your heart to send the message to your mind that you and your body are safe. When you feel safe, all of your body systems relax and let go of the residual fight-or-flight syndrome that we all carry with us. Most of us are ready to jump at anything most of the time. We are always on edge. When we think about being still, our minds run through the litany of all the reasons why we can't. But when our breathing and hearts slow and are not under stress, our hearts tell our brains, "We are safe; just chill!" The body and mind will listen. Really, the heart, as its beats slow, tells the brain the body is okay, and the brain tells the body to chill, as it's okay and safe, and it does!

Aura Colors

Q. I know our chakras have different colors. Why? I can see them now and then when I am calm and just sitting there. Sometimes I can see a color glow around someone. I know people have energy, but why colors?

A. As we have spoken about before, we are energy. Energy is vibration. Energy is movement. Movement has different frequencies. Each of our chakras vibrates at a different frequency, and therefore the chakras project different colors. Each frequency vibrates at a different speed and creates different colors, depending on the speed or rate of vibration. This energy field vibrates at the correct levels to energize our bodies and each of our organs. When all of our frequencies are at the correct speed, we are healthy and happy. When our colors are wobbly or slow, we become ill. It may also be that when we become ill, our frequencies, and therefore our colors, change. (We are not sure what comes first, the chicken or the egg!) We can feel the change within us. Sometimes it's caused by what we eat or how we live, and very often it's caused by how we manage or understand our emotions. If our thinking and feelings are dark, hateful, fearful, or mean, we cannot glow or sparkle, giving off our positive current to others. We become dark and ill. As we fall into depression, it is difficult to move back into the light. We can control much of our energy by how we think and what we believe. We have all heard the old adage, "If you think you can, you are right! If you think you can't, you are right!" What and how we think majorly impact our health at all levels, and therefore our thoughts impact our vibrations and colors, and that, in turn, affects our physical bodies at all levels.

We all have colors. Our colors are called auras. Our auras are made up of different energy frequencies that emanate from our bodies' electrical systems. This was proven by the work of Semyon Davidovich Kirlian, a Russian quantum physicist, in the 1950s and 1960s. He developed a way to measure the biofield of any living thing. His work became known as "Kirlian photography."

As soon as the equipment was available to the public, many people started using this method to take pictures peoples' auras at various points in their lives to show how emotions and decisions affect our energy fields. Some people also can feel this energy with their hands. Nowadays, there are computers that can do all this accurately and give you a perfectly understandable, correct readout. Will wonders never cease!

Our bodies are like crystals that take in the white light of the sun and light from the universe and reflect the seven colors of the rainbow back to the universe through our chakra systems. Our pituitary gland, located in the center of our head, is the prism that breaks down the light energy, refracts it, and distributes it to our bodies through our chakras.

The major (we have minor chakras as well in our hands and feet) chakra placements and their colors are as follows:

Brain (top of head)	Violet
Nerves (center forehead or third eye)	Indigo
Respiration: (throat)	Blue
Circulation (heart center)	Green
Nutrition (high stomach area)	Yellow
Secretion (bowel area)	Orange
Generations (end of spine, sex organs)	Red

If you are blessed with the gift of seeing, you understand that we glow and sparkle with the light we shine. This is true—an actual scientific fact. It is not just a thought or belief system but is really real! We are light. Our light and the way in which we think and believe about this gift of light help us and others keep well mentally, physically, emotionally, and spiritually. I hope this was written in an understandable way.

Smudging

Q. What is smudging, and how do you do it?

A. Smudging is a traditional ceremonial ritual for purifying or cleaning out negative energies and thoughts. This spiritual offering is used by indigenous peoples and many others around the world. Smudging is viewed by many as a sacred blessing.

Smudging works by intention. Set your intention before you start. Take a few deep, relaxing breaths to clear the mulligrubs out of your mind and focus on your intention.

Traditionally, we softly speak to the bowl or shell we put our sage or other burnable materials in as we light our material. Holding the bowl over our heads, we offer the smoke to the spirit world or one we may know and believe is supporting us in that world. Then we offer the smoke, holding the bowl in our hands offering our words and smoke to the four directions—north, south, east, and west, asking for the blessings we seek and giving thanks to the spirits and loved ones in each direction. (Do not worry about not having the right bowl or feather or whatever. The important part is one's intention inside, not the outside accommodations.)

The thoughts of energy and intention used by many indigenous peoples around the world are considered by many to be sacred blessings. Our intentions are real and carry power. The smoke helps support our intentions and helps them move through the ethers to bring us to a positive conclusion.

If you collect your own white sage, always leave the root and part of the plant so it will continue to grow and be available for others to offer their requests and blessings to others. Many different plants have been used to smudge. Use what is available and works for you. Many believe that a certain bowl or feathers must be used for this ceremony. Use what you have on hand. Don't make yourself nuts or feel anxious trying to find the right equipment. Remember, energy *is*. It is our intention coupled with our action that creates the energy we are asking for. A kitchen bowl and a leaf will do. Whatever substance you have on hand to create smoke will work. It is our intents, thoughts, and belief systems that make the difference.

Following are some examples of things people say when smudging:

- I cleanse my home of all negativities.
- I am grateful for … Thank you.
- I live in harmony of mind, body, and spirit. Thank you.
- I release all negative energies that do not support me.
- I release conditioned patterns and trust that the universe will support my intentions to guide me.

Crystals

Q. Do crystals really have energy, and why do people use them?

A. Energy is *us!* Energy *is!* It never dies, even when we do. Energy is all there is. It is what we and everything thing on the earth, as well as the earth itself, is made of. Some people call this energy spirit, God, or the creative force. On a scientific level, energy can be seen moving through very powerful microscopes. Even rocks contain moving atoms and even smaller moving particles. But they move so slowly it would take centuries to perceive them as moving. All life is energy, even if we don't think of it as life. Trees have life and moving energy. Everything has atoms, and smaller moving particles, invisible to the eye, that work together. Live energy, such as people and animals, moves faster and is more complex than plant energy and other types of energy. It has been proven in scientific studies that trees can perceive and react to something being in pain around them. Some years ago, there was a study at Duke University that proved this. They no longer do this work, and I have not been able to find the original experiments, but I do remember when it came out publicly. A living tree was fitted with electrodes and attached to an electrocardiograph machine. In another room, live shrimp were put into boiling water. The tree reacted at the same moment the shrimp were put into the water. The tree had shown awareness of the sudden death of another living thing. Does that mean the tree had consciousness? I don't know, but it is certainly food for thought. Our native cultures believe that everything has consciousnesses. In many native and aboriginal cultures, the people give thanks before killing anything, including grass, trees, and animals. They thank the Great Spirit or the energy of the living thing for giving up its life for their cause.

What we *think* is energy. Thoughts have the power to move. We have all heard the phrase, "Mind over matter." If we think of crabbiness and discord, that is what will manifest in our lives. If we think of positivity and love, that is what will manifest in our lives. If we think of health, we will overcome many physical issues or not have to deal with them at all. Energy is *us*, through and through. Sometimes what manifests in our lives are things we don't even realize we are asking for with our minds. Our thoughts, our prayers, and our very consciousness are moving energy. Energy moves where we direct it, based on how we think and what our intention is. When we think of calling Betty and she calls us, when we request help through prayer, when a random thought pushes out with strong emotions behind it and it moves toward what we requested or think we want, that is quantum physics at work. This is the simplest explanation we could come up with.

Crystals are found in the soil in many places around the world. They can hold and transmit energy. It has been said that quartz crystals are the most powerful energy holders and transmitters in the world. IBM, Raytheon, and many other companies mine crystals to use in their electronic products. We use them today in our computers, in astrophysics, and in many other ways. Shamans and healers use them in their healing work.

When we cut down a tree, there is still energy in the tree. It changes into heat and light when we burn it; the ashes turn to food for plants, and the smoke rises into the air, allowing potash to fall back to the earth to help plants grow. In former cultures, it was used to tan hides. We still smoke meat with wood smoke today. It is all energy in different forms. Many believe that this world and the encompassing energy is certainly part of what God is. God is within as well as without, in all ways. Energy *is*. It never dies. It only changes form, just as we do. Each to his or her own belief.

Q. Can people really see into a crystal ball?

A. "Scrying" is an old name for "crystal gazing," or gazing into the future with the aid of a crystal ball or any object that can reflect the pictures in our minds.

Perhaps the first reference to "gazing" any of us remember encountering is that of the mirror on the wall and the question "Who's the fairest one of all?" From Disney's *Snow White and the Seven Dwarfs*. That animated film was released in 1938! Wow, that's even older than I am! Research shows us that even the Druids and many early people used still ponds to "see." As time went on, shiny metal plates or any smooth, clear reflective objects were used. Often people would use toning sounds—what we might today call a mantra or chant—as a way to calm their bodies and minds into balance, bringing deep relaxation and clarity to mind and body. They learned that this helped their minds open and allowed them to "see" from within.

Although it would seem as though the pictures formed in the objects they were working with, the pictures were actually in their minds. In many cultures, this practice was considered evil or witchcraft, and it was only properly accessible by the shamans or healers of the day. People did not realize that what they were seeing was not actually inside the objects they were using to "see." The objects were only points that they focused their minds on as they mentally requested information, and their bodies and minds became stilled so they could focus on the visions they were having. Most people in former times, except the village shaman or healer, did not understand the use of a quiet mind and how, when our minds stop jumping around, we receive information relating to the energetic world around us. These truths were taught only to those who would be healers or shamans—priests in their communities. The information was often passed down through family lines, as some family groups had finer abilities than others to work with the energies.

When our minds are calm, we can learn to control them, learning to pick up many other kinds of energy. As we are able to learn this, we are more able to "see" what might happen next in our lives. As we have said before, everything is energy. Energy is movable. We can learn how to control our minds and bodies to feel and see different levels of energy. In former times, since very few people were aware of this information, only the trained— priests and such—were able to study and use these abilities. It was considered evil for others to know such things. Now we know and can prove that the abilities some people have cultivated are part of our God given gifts and part of how we understand science (or the understanding the creative forces). It has been proven by medical science that we can control our minds and emotions. We have free will to think and act in ways both positive and negative, helpful and damaging. We can pick up on energy that is part of someone else, such as when you know Jim, who hasn't called in a year, is going to call. Man, you have been thinking of him all day! And wouldn't you know it, he calls! Or perhaps you just know a business deal will work a certain way, and it does!

Think about all the times you lay on the lawn as a kid, just relaxing and being a bit silly, perhaps with your friends or parents, as you watched the clouds overhead go by and saw a turtle or horse or boat just floating by and changing shape as you focused on the clouds. You focused on what you were seeing. Your mind, open to the adventure and whatever shape came into your sight, would connect the shape to something you already knew. You knew what a boat and a horse looked like. Your mind just helped you identify something that could never be in the sky. You knew it wasn't really a boat or horse in the sky, but your mind gave you the insight to "see" a representation of the object. Scientifically, the name for this is "pareidolia."

So, without any fancy words or "spells" or anything, as we are looking into a ball, a crystal, a glass of water, a pond, or a cup of coffee or tea when our minds are relaxed, we, too, can see imagined things in the object we are using to see with. As we ask questions and watch in a relaxed way, an answer often appears. It takes practice, but these ideas are gifts we all have. Most of us don't use them or even realize that they were given to us as part of our spiritual development.

Cards

Q. How do people read cards?

A. I have been reading cards for over fifty years. I started with playing cards and then checked out different types of tarot cards. Morgan Greer was one that spoke to me, and I have kept the same deck since then. I tried to learn from a book, but what works for me is just being calm and asking the card what it could mean. As an answer comes, I write it down; and the next time I read, I check with the written answers. Over the years, I have understood what the cards are telling me. But this is not because I learned in a book. They can speak to us individually, and over time we will remember. Regular playing cards work the same way. The knowledge comes from our "within," or our Innate—that part of us that knows everything. It's always better if we learn on our own and learn to speak the language of our cards from our inner selves.

Tarot, as most of us understand, is a very old system—centuries old. Every country or culture has tarot or some version of passing hidden knowledge. The word "occult" means "hidden knowledge," not "bad" or "evil." In the past, rulers, kings, emperors, and such believed that people could not have certain esoteric knowledge. In some points in our world history, it was considered forbidden knowledge. The knowledge was taken underground. Many played games of chance as a pastime, and secret knowledge was hidden within the cards or dice, with each number or card face offering clues to the secret lesson to be learned. Who would know? The information to the initiates would still get out, and training could be done undercover. What if regular people realized that they could, through using the power of their consciousness and minds, elevate pain? What if people could individually reach out to their Creator or "guides" without assistance from a priest or holy person, or learn how to fly by leaving their bodies? Why would they need an iron-fisted ruler? How could anyone control them? See the problem?

That is one of the reasons playing cards have always had such a negative reputation over the years. Some of the ideas of secrecy stuck, and over time people forgot that the negative feelings about playing card games were a way to control people. If it was illegal to play cards and get the information woven into their pictures and art, practitioners would just go underground, and the information would become truly hidden.

People use tarot cards or regular playing cards for divination, meaning looking for unknown future knowledge for themselves or others, self-guidance, meditation, and spiritual development. In reality, this information comes from within. The cards are only paper and ink. But the pictures help our minds focus and tickle the subconscious to help bring information to the surface.

I use the Morgan Greer deck when I read because they were a gift to me over fifty years ago, and they speak to me. There are many, many different cards on the market these days. You will have to see which ones speak to you. Learning to understand them, once you choose, is the same method used to learn anything—repetition. However, we must not just learn what books and teachers say; rather, we need to recognize information that naturally comes to us. As we work with the cards, we will realize that thoughts and pictures will just come out of the blue. They just show up in our minds. As we learn to relax and let the energy flow, we will need the cards to work with less and less. Learning to use the cards is also training our minds to reach out beyond our five senses.

Personally, I don't need cards to read, as I am an empath and medium. But the cards help me focus so I can bring up better information. Sometimes I pick up a card and know it relates to someone connected to the receiving person who has passed. Then I bring through the message from that person's loved one.

In reading cards, like everything else, information comes upon request from your inner self, or your Innate.

Following is an old story that you may enjoy. I believe the original is taken from a World War I story. The author is unknown. This is taken from my self-published 2021 book *Simply Cards: A Guide to Reading Playing Cards*. (You can contact me if you are interested in the book. Copies are available only through my office currently.)

A Soldier's Story

A soldier attending worship service with the rest of the regiment at a church in Glasgow, England, instead of pulling out a Bible like the others, pulled out a deck of playing cards. This behavior did not pass unnoticed by the pastor or the sergeant of the company. The sergeant requested he put away the cards. When the soldier refused, he was taken before the mayor, and the sergeant presented a formal complaint for the soldier's indecent behavior during church services. "Well, soldier!" said the mayor, "What excuse have you for this strange scandalous behavior? If you can make any apology or assign any reason for it, it's well. If you cannot, assure yourself that I will cause you to be severely punished for it!"

"Since Your Honor is so good," replied the soldier, "I will inform you. I have been eight days on march, with a bare allowance of sixpence a day, which Your Honor will allow is hardly sufficient to maintain a man in meat, drink, washing, and other necessaries that consequently he may want, without a Bible, prayer book, or any other good book."

On saying this, the solder drew out his pack of cards and, presenting one of the aces to the mayor, continued his address to the magistrate as follows:

"When I see an ace, may it please Your Honor, it reminds me that there is only one God. And when I look upon a two or a three, the former puts me in mind of the Father and Son, and the latter of the Father, Son, and Holy Ghost. A four calls for remembrance of the four evangelists, Mathew, Mark, Luke, and John. A five, the five wise virgins who were ordered to trim their lamps; there were ten, indeed, but five, Your Worship may remember, were wise, and five were foolish. A six reminds me that in six days God created heaven and the earth. A seven, that on the seventh day he rested from all that he had made. An eight, of the eight righteous persons preserved from the deluge: Noah and his wife, with his three sons and their wives. A nine, of the nine lepers cleansed by our Savior; there were ten, but only one returned to offer his tribute of thanks. And a ten, of the Ten Commandments that God gave Moses on Mount Sinai, on the two tablets of stone."

He took the knave and put it aside.

"When I see the queen, it puts me in mind of the queen of Sheba, who came from the furthermost parts of the world to hear the wisdom of Solomon. She was as wise a woman as he was a man, for she brought fifty boys and fifty girls all clothed in girls' apparel to show before King Solomon, for him to test which were boys and which were girls. But he could not tell until he called for water for the children to wash themselves. The girls washed up to their elbows, and the boys only up to the wrists of their hands, so King Solomon told by that. And when I see the king, it puts me in mind of the Great King of Heaven and Earth, which is God Almighty."

"Well," said the mayor, "You have given a good description of all the cards except one, which is lacking."

"Which is that?" asked the soldier.

"The knave," said the mayor.

"If Your Honor will not be angry with me," returned the soldier. "I can give you the same satisfaction on that as any in the pack."

"No," said the mayor.

"Well ..." replied the soldier. "The greatest knave that I know is the sergeant who brought me before you."

"I don't know whether he be the greatest knave or not," the mayor replied, "but I am sure that he is the greatest fool."

The soldier then continued as follows:

"When I count the number of dots in a pack of cards, there are 365—as many days as there are in a year. When I count how many cards are in a pack, I find there are fifty-two—as many weeks as are in a year. When I reckon how many tricks are won by a pack, I find there are twelve—as many months as there are in a year. So, this pack of cards is Bible, almanac, and prayer book to me."

★★★

I hope this story has opened some doors for you in whatever way it was meant to.

And when the Seven Thunders had uttered their voices, I was about to write but I heard a voice from Heaven saying unto me, "Seal up those things, uttered by Seven Thunders, and write them not." And I took the little book out of the angel's hand and devoured it; and to my taste it was sweet as honey, but as soon as I devoured it, it became bitter unto my inside. And he said unto me, "You must prophecy again, before many peoples and nations and tongues and kings." (Revelations 10:4, 10–11).

One of the first known books about Divination using a deck of playing cards is the *Mystic Test Book* by Mr. Olney Richmond, published in 1893. Mr. Richmond was at the time the grand master of a secret society known as the Order of the Magi. He believed that this order was instructed, since the days of Egypt, to keep the secrets of the cards alive and protected. Mr. Richards believed that the above passage reveals that the "little book" is our deck of fifty-two cards, which may have links to Christianity and other ancient esoteric groups. He believed that the cards must have originated in Atlantis, since all major civilizations claim their invention. The word "magic" comes from the word "Magi," which refers to the Wise Men who followed the star during the birth of Jesus.

> Who Knows how and why card reading started??
> Your adventure will start with you figuring it out!

Reiki

Q. What is Reiki?

A. Reiki is an ancient and profoundly simple system of the laying on of hands. This touch-healing system was introduced to us from Tibetan Buddhism. Reiki is not a religion. It is a healing process developed in Tibet and Japan over thousands of years. It is a process to help us clear our minds or centers and calm ourselves and focus on the Creator's given life force with the intention that God's will be done, or on the "higher good," similar to advanced or focused prayer. I always ask for the higher good to be done. I don't know my clients' paths, so asking for the higher good does not have me asking for something that cannot be. Once the practitioner is calm and focused, his or her hands may become hot or feel tingly through the act of concentration and intent. Hands are then placed above the injured or ill area of the body. There does not need to be physical contact. It can be offered direct or in person, or it can occur over long distances, just as people use prayer for someone who is not near them.

The first thing people realize during and after a Reiki session is profound relaxation, which often helps create a diminishment of pain that can last for days and weeks. In some cases, the pain or illness never returns.

We cannot make any claims that Reiki cures anything, but we know—and traditional medicine will support this—that as the body is able to relax, it is better able to help heal any issues, be they physical, emotional, mental, or spiritual. As the body relaxes, the mind relaxes and releases the terrible grip of fear, which hinders any kind of healing process. Fear is the emotion that holds us back and creates illness in our minds and bodies. When I'm in a session with someone I always ask my guides for help, calmness, and support in allowing the energy to flow without any personal blockages I may have without realizing it. I personally ask for the energy to be used for the highest good. I'm not a doctor. I may not know the correct specifics of the situation. But in asking for help for the highest good to take place, I am not directing the energy to a place that may not be on the person's path. The highest good may be something I would never know. I act as the supporting intermediary, not the healer. Our Creator and the creative force of our Innate heals.

I have worked in the holistic health field for over fifty years, and I'm so pleased that at last traditional and nontraditional medicine can work together as integrated healing. Years ago I started my professional career by learning and teaching therapeutic touch, along with methods I learned as a child from my grandfather, who was a hands-on healer and a holistic family doctor.

As always, we never advocate dismissing one's traditional medical practitioner. We believe in combined therapies that encompass all the physical, mental, and spiritual attributes of healing. Also, we urge you to never stop a medically directed therapy or medication without discussing your situation and beliefs with your primary care person. All healing starts with your intent and a calm mind.

Therapeutic touch was a popular persecutor to Reiki that was popular in the 1970s. It is a laying-on-of-hands process similar to Reiki that is used to move energy. At one time, most hospitals had incorporated this method into their nursing systems. Therapeutic touch was developed by Dolores Krieger, PhD, RN, of New York University's Division of Nursing, and Dora Kunz, a natural healer. I was lucky enough to study under these women.

Q. How can I find a reader?

A. I would say this should be done with care! If the person is someone you are researching or someone a friend tells you about, pay attention to what he or she says and how he or she responds to you. There are many of us who read very well and are trustworthy, but others are looking only to make lots of bucks! Seekers who portray themselves as distressed or lonely are marks and may go down a very bad road with someone they don't know and really have no clue about. Also, beware of people who have "overly spiritual" names, such as Bill Light Bringer or Sally Angel. I would also advise caution with someone who insists he or she is bringing a special message from Saint So-and-So just for you. Sorry, but if Saint So-and-So had a real message for you, don't you think he or she would know how to reach out to you himself or herself? I mean, a saint can come and go through any physical or nonphysical medium he or she is in! Why would a saint have to go through a reader to give you information he or she had for you? Use common sense!

If there is any hint of the person pushing you to be fearful, *run*. You want someone who has the skills to be truthful, clear, and a bringer of light. That doesn't mean you want someone who will tell you only good things. Only you can truly know whether he or she is reading you correctly. No authentic person will ever tell you something like "At 2:00 p.m. tomorrow, be aware of crossing the street. I'll send you a talisman for protection, for just the cost of postage," implying that something bad could happen. People who have a true gift of discernment need not be threatening. If someone tells you that you are at the dawn of a new life but that to be successful you need to agree to let him or her help you so you can become successful and seize all the possibilities that come your way, *run!* If someone is pushing you to contact him or her because he or she *knew* you were going to call him or her, because he or she saw you in his or her dream, or because he or she just knew you would reach out, and so forth, *run*. If someone says, "I knew you were going to contact me, so I made a video just for you so I would be ready when you reached out. You are not alone, my dear. Don't worry; I am here to guide you!" or if someone tells you to stick with him or her because he or she sees you winning the lottery and claims to have been given the special numbers just for you but asks for some small token because he or she has to pay for various things to be able to offer you lifesaving, family-healing, and income-producing knowledge, *run*. A legitimate reader would never talk to you in that way. This kind of thing happened to me recently. I was just checking on someone, and the person used many of these lines on me. If that person had really been reading me, he would have had a clue, but he obviously did not.

When you choose someone, you think will fit for you, there may be a fee for time and energy spent, within a normal range. Check around and see what the going price is in your area. Most of the readers in this country that I know of charge about one dollar per minute as of the publication of this book. Readings often last half an hour. When I read from my office, I ask for a flat rate and do not count the minutes. This is the case even if I'm reading by phone. I read until the reading is done (when the energy stops). If I'm doing a show or home party, my rates are lower. But in those cases, I have a time frame I must fit people into. If I'm doing gallery readings, I often just ask people to donate. It depends on the situation and whether I'm doing a fundraiser for a group or not. So it varies. I discourage parents from bringing their children in for readings. Readings are serious, and children do not understand them. When I do read for a child because the parents insist, I make sure I say only positive things that will guide the child. If a child tells me he or she likes math, for example, I can say something positive about how smart the child is. I would never give a child a negative reading or discourage or upset him or her in any way. With a child, you can always find positive, appropriate possibilities. As mediums or psychics, we get information from the person we are reading for by way of energy exchange. This means that when I read, I pick up feelings and pictures from a person's energy vibration. Being a medium as well, I also at times can pick up information from a person's loved ones who have passed. These processes are also part of quantum science.

All of us have gifts that guide us. But most of us have never learned how to use them. When I'm teaching a group of students, they are often surprised at the skills they have but never realized they have.

Divorce

Q. What do you think happens to you spiritually when you divorce?

A. No one has ever asked us a question like that, so I have done some research on your question. There are others who have more insight and knowledge than we have on this very personal and in-depth matter.

I have paraphrased an answer from Kryon Masters, which I received in July 2021. If you are interested, you can find his channel and his wisdom on YouTube and elsewhere on the internet. He also has about seventeen books out that will provide an eye-opening view into the world of spirit. Following is what he has to say about divorce; I think it's very enlightening. I think anyone with plans to start a partnership might do well to read and understand another pathway in relationships. The same goes for anyone who has made these difficult decisions and is still looking for healing. Separating a partnership can be an extremely painful process that may take a very long time to heal. If we could follow this path, there would be much less pain and anger in our world. I think perhaps we all need to learn to be a bit more mature about these things. But then most do not look at partnerships in this way.

When the energy and consciousness of one are in a different reality from those of the other and it's obvious that this will never change, it may be the time to make that decision. This isn't about enlightenment. It's obvious that will never change. It is about our personal individual paths. Although contrary to our society, the rules of the church, and what our families wish for us, sometimes we go through partnership stages that are appropriate but temporary. This can also occur between two enlightened souls who simply needed to be together for a while.

So, if we are going to separate a partnership, we should do it with integrity, do it in a way in which we offer friendship, and do it with maturity and wisdom. Never slam the door. We can offer the other person our maturity all our life and always give him or her the opportunity for forgiveness and discussion.

As we grow older, we will eventually see the dynamics of growth and the reasons why a temporary partnership might have been needed in our own personal path or in theirs. Sometimes such a partnership is only a placeholder keeping people in place so that something else can happen.

Each path is different, and there are as many who will stay together until they hold hands again on the other side. Then they will do it again the next time around. Don't pass judgment either way. There is appropriateness in many things that result in growth and maturity for either or both.

I hope this is an answer that makes sense to you, and that its truth fits in your heart. If you are interested, you can contact Kryon at info@KryonMasters.com.

I wish someone had taught me this way of thinking and caring when I was much younger. Just think how all of our lives would change if we could all learn this. We don't need to keep creating so much grief for ourselves and others. We can learn to let go, focus on love, move on, and not judge.

Holistic Health

Q. I believe in holistic health. I grow my own herbs, don't eat meat, and grow most of my own vegetables. My husband insists I see a doctor for a condition I have, but I feel as if I would be cheating if I were to do that. What do you think?

A. I think you are admirable to grow your own food and to pay attention to what may hurt your body. I think herbs and fresh food are important. I see doctors and the traditional medical field as another arm we have been given to support us. As we have said throughout, energy *is*. We are all connected. I grow many herbs, use them, and offer them to others. I have been doing this work for many years. I have been part of the traditional health-care system as well. Where do you think our medical supporters learned what they know? They had the God-given brains, insight, and drive to study and learn as much as was available in the world of medicine and science at the time, in the field they were drawn to. Medicine and science are not separate from the whole. (It's *all* connected!) There is nothing wrong with working with a trained and knowledgeable medical team. They are here to support us no matter what our personal beliefs may be. I am blessed that I have a doctor who hears, listens, digests, and makes supportive and knowledgeable comments and helps me make decisions about my health and care. When I say I don't think a certain medication is good for me because I did muscle testing and the test said I should not take the prescription because it's too strong, he listens and adjusts my medications without a fuss. We may discuss my findings and understanding and his learning, but we always work it out in sensible ways. If he believes I am not correct in my thinking, we discuss it and come to an agreement to test the theories. I no longer think I'm always right! I learned the hard way. I told him recently that he may even know more than I do! We have also been working together for over ten years. He knows me and Ed. We trust him. So, I would suggest you find a doctor you are comfortable with and that will be able to work with you over a long period—someone who will listen to your words and will do some research to see whether you are both on the same page.

Do your research so you can speak with some knowledge about your situation. Be ready with any suggestions and be willing to look at different aspects that you may not see or understand up front.

Enlightenment

Q. Can you tell me what "enlightenment" really means? I hear it all the time, but I have no real clue.

A. Here are the suppositions we came up with through our work. We hope these words are helpful in your search.

When we look at our world, people, animals, earth, and the universe, it all connects. If we believe that our universe was created by a Creator and was not just a crazy happenstance accident, then perhaps we can put our lives into a more positive and understandable plan of consciousness. It is our choice. We were given a brain to think, a body to make our world tangible, and emotions to help us understand how others feel and think.

Looking at science, we see that the universes at all levels are connected by mathematics, meaning high-level quantum physics or quantum mechanics. It doesn't matter if any of us really understand this stuff. It works whether we believe it and understand it or not. It is in the quiet that we find peace and the understanding we need. Just know it's all connected. Everything is numbers and vibrations of those numbers that connect in many ways with everything, balanced, equal, and sense-making. From our DNA to the farthest galaxy, it all connects. We can all look at creation as totally amazing!

In the old Newtonian physics, we learned in school, everything was based on action and reaction. Every action creates an opposite and equal reaction. That is still true, but wait, there's more! Physics is the study of movement—how and why things move.

This covers hitting a ball, driving a car, and blowing up a balloon. How and why does something move? What are the components that make it do so? These can include air pressure, gravity, and everything else that would have even a minuscule effect on movement. Quantum physics is basically the study of the how and why of particles too small to be seen by the human eye. These bits that can think, or seem to have a consciousness, bring light that moves, as well as sounds, and they can be directed by our thoughts, as well as run around on their own and organize our entire universe! An experiment at CERN in Switzerland proved that by the simple act of someone observing a photon (a tiny packet of light) move, the photon "realized" it was being observed and changed its expected direction. This is called the double slot experiment. You can go to the CERN website and check for yourself if you have the interest. There is so very much that we still need to trust because we do not yet have the capacity to grasp the enormity of our world and how we affect its interactions in every way.

Many believe that the reason we are here is to learn and to purify our thinking and our responses to others as we evolve on our paths.

Following, presented in a rather simplistic way, are some of the insights we have gathered through our search for enlightenment and understanding.

We were created by a powerful force. This force always was, and it will never leave. We humans cannot wrap our minds around this concept. We are linear in this life and find it difficult to understand a multidimensional existence. Quantum physics is multidimensional. Our understanding of this force is that our Creator is multidimensional and never-ending. This force runs the universes and everything we think we know—which, in reality, is nothing. The whole is so vast that we humans at this time cannot wrap our minds around it all. This force, which we call "God" or other names, is always within us. We have free will to work with this force or not.

God loves us. The only word we have in the English language to describe that feeling and knowing is the word "love." That does not even hold a candle to the power that this energy is and bestows on us.

Think of this: there are nearly eight billion people on Earth. The majority believes in a creator. We pray and ask for what we need or want as we are taught to. Our Creator "receives and hears" every prayer anyone offers 24–7 and knows all our names and situations. Ask even if you don't believe the same as others or think you don't believe in God. The creative force "gets it." We were made by and are part of the force. Don't ever give up. If a request comes truly from your heart, it doesn't matter. The creator is always there, and we are never abandoned even on our darkest night of the soul. Prayers are directed thoughts. They are not necessarily thoughts that follow a script. The essence of the script is what the masters have taught. Prayers are always answered, even if the answers are not what we want. Many of us have never learned how to receive. We don't understand how important it is to be quiet and listen. We ask, and we then promptly get up and walk away, and we wonder that we don't get an answer. Perhaps learning to pay better attention would be helpful.

Our scripture tells us that God is within. What does that really mean? To us it means we are always with God (or whichever word or words we use to name this force). God is always with us. We can ask for any information we need about any decisions we make, and the answer is given, every time. The key is to sit in quiet to hear. Only we can decide what it means for us to sit in quiet and ask and then listen. Some of us forget to listen and wonder why we don't get an answer. Sometimes the answer comes as an insight we suddenly receive, and it blows our minds.

Our Creator made us. Don't you think "He" has a clue about how people are and what they think, as well as what makes them happy, sad, fearful, angry, or in love? We are humans. We were made and placed here by our Creator. Do you really think this great force would be upset by what we may call it or how we decide to give thanks to this force? We have no inkling, for the most part, how large our Creator is. Fussing about not using the right pronoun is *not* part of the package! We think there are more important things to be concerned about. Every culture has its own ways and names. None are wrong. Some ideas may be displaced as a result of wrong thinking, but then the force already knows that. It's not our problem. A larger hand than ours is dealing with it.

Our emotions are like a barometer. All the emotions that we have, we have for a reason. They give us a clue about how we see the world. Do we need to look at other insights? Do we see the connection between ourselves and others? Our emotions are a direct link to our learning and healing of ourselves and others, as well as our understanding of the universal energies. We believe this earth is our school. When we graduate, we will move on and adjust to what we learned; and when the time is right and we are healed, we will return in some way to continue our journey of helping the force and doing our part.

The most important thing is that through our emotions we connect with others and other things—even things that many of us don't think about, such as the earth itself. Our indigenous peoples around the world knew this. Many practiced giving thanks when they had things and giving thanks for things they previously had in the past. A rain dance is not about making it rain; a rain dance is a giving of thanks for the rain that was given in the past. By offering thanks for this gift, more will come. The ceremony offers thanks and appreciation, opening the way for better to come.

The more we recognize our own emotions, the more we relate to others. The more we relate to others, the more we can choose to bring about peace. We have all experienced peace, pain, love, broken hearts, sadness, grief, fear, and all of the other emotions we have. Animals feel some of our emotions as well. Look at our pets. They experience our love and give back unconditional love. We know they do. When they have not been traumatized, they bring only love. They are gifts to us. We were given emotions as a learning tool not by accident, but on purpose. By feeling emotions, ourselves, we learn, at some point, what we want to help others feel and understand what is and is not helpful to our growth or theirs. We have felt pain; if we understand that, it is within our purview to bring pain or healing to others. Most of us would choose to bring positive, supporting words and healing actions to others.

We have all experienced these emotions. We all know what they feel like. As we interact with others, we can just say what we think or feel without regard for the feelings of others and what light or darkness we may be spreading into another life. Since we can all understand emotions, because we have all felt them, we have a responsibility to rethink our pain and how we affect others' emotional fields. Since we have felt both supportive and destructive emotions, we can consciously choose not to bring negative feelings to others. When we have a true working understanding of the impact, we have on life itself, we may consider ourselves to be on an enlightened pathway.

Our lives are a team sport. Everyone is welcome and is affected and supported by what happens to the whole. This is our school and our laboratory. We are learning together. There is always hope. We will always reach a positive end … in time. We have the capacity and ability if we have the desire.

By pulling back the curtain of universal changes in belief systems, power plays among nations, cultures, and governments on the earth over centuries, we can see the truth and act on it. We are of God. We are part of God. God is within us, and we live forever. (Energy never can be destroyed; it only changes form, as we'll do as we learn we will walk with God.) As Yoda says, "May the force be with you!"—not the lightsaber, but the *true force!* I saw a sign the other day that said, "You think you have it bad, think of 'Him' who holds up the universe." Sorry, but our Creator is the Universe—all of it!

Enlightenment is finally *knowing* we are *all* of God and we are loved always.

Chakras

Q. What are the spinning wheels people talk about when they talk about energy?

A. Another word for energy wheels is "chakras." The word "chakra" means "vortex" or "spinning wheel" in the Sanskrit language. Chakras can be found on the front and back of your body, along your spine, and on top of your head and your forehead. There are seven main chakras. They are invisible to the human eye, and their size is about the size of a small coin. They have been described as energy portals, or places where energy can enter your body. Chakras respond to vibrations as well as thought (as thought is also a vibration). Musical tones are vibrations at specific frequencies. Each chakra responds to its own frequency. We have seven major Chakras and several smaller ones in the palms of our hands and the soles of our feet.

One way of understanding the function of the chakra system is to see chakras as the link between the physical nervous systems in our bodies and the universal energy that is present everywhere in the universe. Chakras form the connecting link that allows this immaterial universal energy to enter our material physical bodies. When this energy enters our bodies, it is carried by our nervous systems to the places where we most need it. There is a very close borderline between mind and matter, or mass and energy.

Although there is very little mention of chakras in conventional medicine, they form an integral part of our bodies' energy and nervous systems. The reason so little is mentioned about them in conventional medicine is that they are not visible to the naked eye, even though a microscope. Chakras exist in the realm lying between the physical realm and the nonphysical realm. That is precisely where their function lies—in transforming immaterial universal energy into physical energy in your body that can be used to help our bodies' natural healing processes.

7 Chakras

The seventh chakra, the crown, is at the top of the head, toward the back. Its colors are violet, gold, and white. This is where the universe connects to you. This point connects us with universal knowledge and wisdom. It is the area of integration of one's total personality with life and the spiritual aspects of humankind. It is instrumental in experiencing faith and trust, is usually the place where we enter and leave our bodies and is our connection to all that is. It responds to the tone of B.

The sixth chakra, the third eye, lies between the eyebrows, about one inch above the bridge of the nose. Its color is indigo blue. This is the system's psychic center, and it regulates sixth-sense perception, abstract intuition (thinking without thought), and clairvoyance (seeing without seeing). This chakra supports the capacity to visualize and understand mental concepts and the ability to carry out ideas in a practical way. It responds to the tone of A.

The fifth chakra, the throat, is at the center of the throat and rear of the base of the neck. Its color is blue. The throat center works with communication on all levels and with feelings of self-worth. This center assists with the abilities and issues of physical and nonphysical communication and hearing. This is the center of creative expression for communication between the being and personality (inner voice) of telepathy and clairaudience (communicating with others at a direct thought level and "hearing" the thoughts of other people.) It is also the expression of truth and the ability to listen to one's inner voice. It responds to the tone of G

The fourth chakra, the heart, is at the center of the chest Its colors are pink and green. This is the system of love in all forms: love of self, others, planet, universe, and forgiveness. This is the transition point between body and being. The physical body directs chakras 1 through 3 through conscious and subconscious thoughts, rest, and nutrition. One's being or energy self directs chakras five through seven through subconscious thoughts. The heart chakra supports functions of self-esteem and feelings of security. It responds to the tone of F.

The third chakra, the solar plexus, is at the center of the body where the ribs begin to spread. Its color is yellow. This is where you connect yourself to the universe. The solar plexus distributes energy throughout your body. It carries functions of will and personal strength, as well as power levels. It holds information about getting in and out of the body, remembers what we do when we're out of our bodies, and acts as the body's energy center.

121

It can also be the seat of creativity. The energy of the Solar Plexus also supports us with outwardly projected energies, ambition, and personal power. It responds to the tone of E.

The second chakra, the belly, is at the center of the body between the underwear line and belly button. Its color is orange. Here is where we hold and insulate emotional trauma. This is the source of sexuality, healing, reproduction, desire, emotion, and gut instincts. It responds to the tone of D.

The first chakra, the root, is at the base of the spine, in the groin, between the anus and genitals. Its color is deep red. This is the survival chakra. It deals with issues of physical survival, survival of the species, grounding, physical energy and vitality, and the ability to anchor ideas and creativity into being. The root charka responds to the tone of C.

The resonant sound that has appeared in all countries and societies in our entire world since as far back as we can investigate, concerning our energy centers, is the sound of om. Om is all vowel sounds (a, e, i, o, u) said at one time. The vibration of om is 110 Hz. It is thought to be the same sound as a whale makes, though I am not sure of the species. This is just an interesting connection.

Near-Death Experiences

Q. Do you think it's true that people can die and come back, like, right away?

A. Many times, people under anesthesia and people having near-death experiences (NDAs) report that they looked down and saw their bodies lying there. Sometimes they can remember and repeat conversations that took place in the OR while they were "out," even though the anesthesiologist said they were unconscious. Many also report that they saw and felt a beautiful peaceful place with many people, friends, and relatives who had passed, and that they felt they were given a choice of whether to stay or leave. The experiences they described were peaceful, beautiful, and filled with love. They never had a fear of death again. I can personally attest to that. I drowned when I was about twelve. It was the most beautiful experience I ever had. I was never afraid to die after that. For me it was just like stepping into another room.

I believe I died, But I have no proof. I was a child about twelve to thirteen years old. Some people have said it was only oxygen deprivation. I have no idea and have no way of doing any research on it at this point. I am happy to share my story, as I believe it. You will have to make your own decision. According to my belief system, I firmly believe it is possible. I know that we are all connected and that we never die; we just change form. Energy *is*, and it cannot be destroyed. It changes form, as we all do. Energy is what all of the universe, as well as everything on this earth, is made of. Energy is vibration, sound, and light. Energy is alive.

I grew up in the country in the state of Maine. One summer weekend, our parents took us to a friend's lakeside cabin to go swimming. There were six of us at the time. Our dad was ex-military and a great swimmer. Our mom had practiced for the Olympic swim team before the war. Both parents were world-class swimmers. Me? Not so much. I could dogpaddle, though! (My dad taught me how to float, so I was never fearful of water, even though I couldn't swim yet.) We always had access to water—farm ponds, streams, and such—but none of us swam well. We mostly just paddled around. Our dad would throw us into the water way over our heads, and we would dog-paddle like crazy to get back to shore, the idea being that we would figure out how to actually swim when we learned not to be scared of being tossed in. There were no such things as swimming lessons back then; people just figured it out. It didn't occur to anyone that we could drown. I mean, we weren't stupid. We would just figure it out!

My turn came to be tossed in again amid all the laughter and silliness that only a bunch of young siblings can create with each other. I remember the feel of cool breeze flashing on my wet skin as I flew through the air and the cold shock of hitting the hard water at cannonball speed. I hit hard. Landing on my back knocked every bit of air out of my lungs. I couldn't move. I was frozen as I sunk into the depths like a rock. I started to struggle, trying to get up and out and find air. The water was black and cold. I was thrashing around, trying to find up. Suddenly a women's voice said loudly, "Stop moving!" I kept thrashing. The voice said louder, with more urgency, "Stop moving now!" I did! I was so scared that if I hadn't been in the water, I would have wet myself! I opened my eyes and saw the most beautiful scene imaginable. Everything was a beautiful, soft light green. As soon as I stopped struggling, I felt calm and peaceful. I was just floating, arms and legs akimbo, perfectly balancing in a blanket of smooth, sparkling, sun-kissed water. The voice was the soft, smooth voice of a lady. She said softly, with kindness, "You will be fine. Stop struggling. You can float!"

Looking around me, I saw the most beautiful tones of blues and greens. Plants were floating up from their anchors in the muck at the bottom of the lake, balancing their delicate leaves on long, swaying stems. Fallen brownish leaves floated through the cool and warm layers like little underwater boats. Tiny air bubbles were swirling around me, catching the light from above, looking like tiny diamonds. Everything looked beautiful and soft. The soft, peaceful voice enfolded me like a warm, silky cocoon. It said, "Don't struggle. You will be okay. If you stay calm, you can move through anything in life." Just then a strong hand grabbed me by the arm and pushed me upward. The next thing I remember is feeling like I had been hit by a brick wall. *Bam!* The ground under me was hard. My dad was doing CPR and breathing into my mouth, trying to save me. Everyone was yelling and making a racket. It was so different from the softness and peace I had just left. Sometimes I think about how nice it will be when it's time to go back.

Did I die? Was it real or was it Memorex (if any of you remember that TV commercial from years ago)? I don't know. The adults there said it was my imagination and that I may have stopped breathing but I didn't die … I have no idea, in truth. But I can tell you that since that day I have never had a fear of dying … ever. If you have no fear, there is no reason you can't continue to do anything you feel is on your path. Without fear, nothing is there to stop you, ever! No one can take that away from you except yourself. I know that all the molecules, photons, and other tiny dots of energy that make us who we are, make our universe, and communicate with us are always around us and in our very cells. This live energy is gifted to us by our Creator.

Another experience I had occurred when my youngest son was an infant. I can only talk about what I experienced. I have no medical information about what happened, I only know what I felt and what I remember. I had pneumonia but did not have the money to go to the doctor. I was so sick I couldn't breathe; I had a high fever and was alone. At one point I left my body and was standing by the side of my bed, watching myself struggling to breathe. I was ready to go. I knew I had a choice. I didn't care. I had given up; I was ready. I couldn't stand the misery and pain. (I'm a wimp at heart.) Then, through a fog, I heard my infant son crying. That was the turning point. I had to come back for my son. Again, I felt as though I had hit a brick wall. I dragged myself out of bed to care for my son. I'm not sure whether I would be here today if he had not started crying. This story is not very dramatic, but it made a believer out of me.

I know that energy can never be destroyed. It just changes form and goes on forever. So that's my story, and I'm sticking to it! We are all free to feel and believe whatever we think about this.

I will add this: although I so miss my little fuzzy guy, I felt happy after he passed because I knew absolutely, he was *not* in pain. When you love someone so much you cannot stand to know he or she is in pain and there is nothing you can do, you are willing to give your own life to put him or her at ease, no matter what. After he passed, he sent a message through a person who also has the gift, even though she did not know either of us. He told her that if he had realized how wonderful it was "over there," he would have left sooner! (The old, learned fears of going to hell for even minor infractions or a bit of wrong thinking were still hiding in the shadows of his youth. He had been ill for a long time. His last three years were very difficult for him. It was fear that kept him here rather than letting him go to where his joy would be.) I know this is true. We had many conversations about these things in the past. I Know!

He also said he knew his life was not perfect. He understood he had made mistakes but now understands how to change that thinking. He is learning a lot so he will be ready when the time for him comes again. He is happy, learning, and productive.

There have been a lot of people who say this has happened to them and have written books about their "travels." Many medical people take these beliefs into consideration, although few will openly agree that this may be so. The only thing I can do is share my personal experience with you. I have been told it was only oxygen deprivation … Who knows? I never saw a doctor, and in the country, there were none around anyway.

Dreams

Q. How can people learn to interpret dreams?

A. We all dream. Sometimes a dream is about a stress in our lives: a fear, real or imagined; something in our lives we need to pay attention to; the room being too hot or cold; or the cat sleeping on your head at 3:00 a.m.!

The first step is to identify the type of dream you are having. Did you eat something that may have been hard to digest? Are your feet too warm or cold? Is someone snoring in the background? Do you recognize your dreams as feelings, pictures, action shots, or still lifes? Are you still or flying and floating?

If you want to remember your dreams, ask your subconscious to let you remember them as you go to sleep. Eventually you will remember most of them. We also suggest you keep a paper and pen on your nightstand. As soon as you wake up, write down what you remember. Dreams have gossamer wings and can flit away before you even remember that you had one! Then one will pop up in the middle of the day, and you will wonder, "Where did that memory come from?" Dreams have a way of poking at us if they involve something we need to know or puzzle out.

Look for metaphors in your dreams. Dreams often come in different forms and most of the time are not straight-out clear pictures. You may have to work to unravel and understand what they are telling you.

A friend gave me a call about a dream a few weeks ago. She had a dream and called to ask what I thought. She dreamed she was in the ocean, with only her head sticking out of the water. She thought she could see a boat in the distance. Looking at each aspect of the dream, this is what I thought: She was in the ocean, but the water was calm, so she was not in danger from storms. Only her head was above the water, which told me she felt she was up to her neck in whatever her situation was. I asked her if there was anything in the water with her. She said no. That told me she felt safe, just kind of waterlogged; there were no sharks or stinging jellyfish that would hurt her. As far as the boat, she could not tell what kind it was, so I asked her what direction the boat was coming from. She said she thought it was coming from the east. Well, a boat could be a form of help, but the east is where the sun or first light comes from. So the arrival of the light told me that the situation would be lightened. The boat and the light suggested help was coming to support her in some way. She would not drown or have dangerous or fearful issues while she was still in the water. She would be okay and would be helped out of the situation.

Looking for metaphors is how I would start learning to interpret your dreams. Our dreams tend to present themselves as metaphors. We all have different metaphors that mean things in our lives, and we can figure them out better than anyone else, because they are ours and come from our subconscious. I would not pay much attention to what others say about your dreams. There are lots of books on the subject, but we are individuals with different life experiences, fears, and loves. Each person's dreams, and indeed each dream, can be a form of guidance. With a little work, we can figure them out.

Tapping

Q. Tapping—what is it?

A. There are many ideas and opinions out there. Much of the traditional research is still out. But in my opinion, self-healing can and does work. For it to work, though, we need to understand how our minds and bodies work together. It's a big subject to try to explain in this short space. I would suggest you learn what you can about different modalities and practice the ones that make sense to you. If you are lucky enough to have a traditional doctor with a nontraditional mind who will listen to you and work with you on your ideas, that's great. If not, make sure you follow the best practices that you can so you are not putting yourself at risk because you may not have understood the full picture.

Crystals, especially quartz crystals, emit energy. We use them in many things, such as watches, computers, and spacecraft. Many times, people respond to the energy a crystal puts out. The vibrations a person encounters work with the body's electrical field and may make the person feel calmer, more relaxed, and just well in general—or they may simply make the person believe he or she feels this way. The funny thing is, our minds don't know the difference between what is real and what is not real. Our minds just know what is right now, and they are guided by our internal feelings and beliefs. One of the self-healing methods I use for myself, and others is called tapping, or the emotional freedom technique (EFT).

We can start with the premise that our bodies are made up of many electrical currents. Each can be reached through the pressure points along our meridian lines, which are like the electrical wall switches in our homes. The transformers outside on the poles are like our brains telling our subconscious where the electric current should flow. If there is a blockage, the power does not run through correctly. Elder medicine men and women called chi masters have taught this throughout the Chinese culture for thousands of years and still use some of these processes today. They call it acupuncture and use hair-fine needles to create a positive energy flow throughout our bodies. I learned many of these techniques when I was in China. Tapping for health is a more modern technique that is like polarity and Reiki therapy. Those methods use energy directed through our hands, minds, and belief systems to help heal. While tapping uses acupressure points and self-implemented mental stimulation and visualization to reach our objectives, it is very easy to learn. Over many years of research and study, the medical field has learned that over time, negative emotions, and feelings may disrupt our bodies' energy, causing anxiety. Something that happened at age two can have an impact throughout someone's life, and the person might never make the connection. But tapping can open the door to healing by helping our energy system rewrite the situation, helping us let go of the stagnating emotion. Our anxiety can stay in our system for the rest of our lives until we learn how to let go of it. Learning tapping is one way to help us and others find the peace we seek.

The anxiety we carry can cause pain in our physical bodies from an accident or a disease, such as arthritis. It can cause emotional pain from our upbringing, time we spent in war, an accident, a highly stressful job, or even what to us could be a terrifying experience even though it may have happened long ago, and we have no current memory of it. That unremembered experience could still cause blockages throughout your body and may be causing pain that could lead to addiction and many other symptoms.

Learning the simple steps of how to use tapping to help us in everyday life is a way of anchoring the words we believe with the ancient pressure points in our bodies. Our bodies and all of their cells will respond to a new way of thinking about ourselves. This will help eliminate the anxiety we feel, which may be causing PTSD or other issues. It does not take long to learn and can be done anywhere. Once you learn the steps and how to direct your words and thinking to work together, you can do it all with your mind.

We are not doctors; nor do we diagnose or prescribe. But we are happy to share with you the knowledge we have learned over decades of life and the teachings of our many wise teachers.

Muscle Testing

Q. What is muscle testing?

A. Muscle testing is in the same category as tapping. It's using your mind and body to get answers about anything pertaining to your mind and body, current or past. Your body does not lie. When you or someone else asks it a question, it cannot lie. The information comes from our subconscious which is also called the Innate. Basically, you can ask a yes-or-no question. Ask someone to hold his or her arm straight out in front of him or her. Have the person take a breath and hold his or her arm firm. Then ask the person to give you his or her name. As the person does so, gently press his or her arm down. Get the feel of what the person's relaxed arm feels like. Now ask the person to give you a name different from his or her own—not his or her real name. Test the arm strength again; this time you should feel the arm as weak. You do not need a lot of pressure to push it down. Once you get the hang of it, you can ask questions like the following: "Did the upsetting event happen before you were five?" "Did someone you know hurt you?" The body knows whether an answer is truthful or not. If you are working with someone else, you can ask the question in your mind, and the person's body will still respond truthfully. You can ask all kinds of things to find out about your health or another's health, or even which food or medication you should or shouldn't take.

I am very blessed to have a doctor who listens. I was prescribed a medication. I checked with muscle testing, asking whether it was correct for me. It said no. I asked, "Why, is it too strong?" The muscle test told me it was. So, I told my doctor what my muscles said, and he changed the scrip. I'm fine. Even though my doctor doesn't use muscle testing in his practice, he knows it works. Many of the AMA's rules do not support holistic health. Many "knowing" medical doctors are limited in their practice because of these regulations. This is an extremely simple explanation. It takes practice and some time, but anyone can learn and use this method. We have had excellent results with PTSD and "unreasonable fear," as well as long-term pain. The best current book on the subject I have found is, *The Emotion Code* by Dr. Bradley Nelson. You can do muscle testing on yourself. This book explains how and how to release the negative emotions or inner pain you may have been feeling.

Muscle testing, tapping, dowsing with a rod or a pendulum, card reading, and the like all use the same process of using inner energy, which is often called the Innate. You use your belief system and your thought process in a relaxed but active way and state what information you need. Remain calm; no wild horses are running around. Just feed 'em and put 'em in the barn; they will quiet down. Or, as my friend Jim from Meditation Warriors says, "Just imagine patting a cat. If you have a real one, pat it. Its purr will help you stay focused. Its purr will start to match your calm energy level and will help you focus on your answer. Let things flow naturally. An answer will come. It will take a bit of practice. Meditation is not meant to torture yourself into staying still. When you first start learning and making this information accessible to your conscious mind, it helps to write things down until you get the 'gist' of it."

Psychics vs. Mediums

Q. What is the difference between a psychic and a medium?

A. Most of us are psychic but don't know it or think of that term when we "Pick something up out of thin air," such as when we get a hunch that we should not take the route we were planning on today and then we find out there was an accident on the road we would have traveled, or when something tells us not to have a relationship with a person and down the road we look back and see what a disaster that relationship would have been for us. We always pick up others' vibrations relating to possible actions and personality. We all do this. Some of us pay attention to this, and some of do not and then kick themselves for not listening! I've been there and done that! I learned the hard way to listen! We say, "Wow! What a coincidence!" or we do something silly like think of someone we haven't seen in a long time just before he or she calls. Wow, what a coincidence! You will see as you read about vibrations that we are connected by energy. Science can prove this. It's not just pie in the sky. All energy, matter, and spirits, seen or unseen, vibrate, and we can and do pick up on this. In our society, people who pick up on that sort of thing correctly are considered psychic. Often the term is used in an offhand silly way, such as when someone says, "Oh, I knew that was going to happen!" with a smile, not really taking it seriously, and someone else replies, "Oh, you must be psychic!" Most of us have never been taught that we are all multidimensional (meaning we are spirit as well as physical, thought as well as emotion). We constantly interact with all parts of ourselves and others both seen and unseen. It's our minds, belief systems, and thinking that can be barriers to that knowledge. We all have these abilities to guide us through life. It's an inner gift that we are all blessed with, but most have no idea.

A medium is also considered psychic. But a psychic is not always a medium. A medium is a person who, mostly, as part of his or her religion, receives messages from loved ones who have passed on. He or she is a medium between one level of existence and another. Often, they bring through a name or personality trait so we can identify who is coming through to us. However, not all mediums are Spiritualists. Spiritualism is a belief that supports the process of receiving information from "beyond." This belief system does not create the process, but it supports those who have this ability, through understanding of our scriptures and science.

Often people from indigenous cultures around the world have these gifts. Native cultures have deep roots in receiving and giving information from past loved ones as well as the insight needed to see possible futures. They understand and have never forgotten that we are all connected to our Creator. All people, plants, animals, rocks, crystals, stars, moons, and suns throughout our universe are connected. We cannot say this enough. Many believe that those who are out of body can connect and guide those who are still in body, especially if there is a strong emotional tie.

We all have these gifts. Most of us have never learned that this is part of who we are or how we can use these gifts to support the greater good. These knowings often run in families but depending on our culture and the time in which we are living, this may not be accepted by everyone.

I have found that many people with these attributes or gifts tend the to follow the Spiritualist belief system because in that system they are accepted for their gifts and are not considered evil or crazy.

Breath

Q. Can you tell me what chi is? Is it the same as prana?

A. Energy comes into our bodies from the air and energy around us and from the earth, through our feet. If you grew up going barefoot a lot, you understand! Anyone who has grown up that way and remembers the feel of earth energy flowing through him or her never loses that feeling of wonderment.

The main function of breathing is to power the rhythmic system of the heart and lungs pumping this life force energy, which enlivens us at every level. It helps us to balance our thinking and feelings, as well as to keep our energy centers or chakras in balance, nurturing every part of our bodies. Have you ever noticed that when you are not getting enough oxygen, your head starts feeling fuzzy? If you are tired and not breathing at full capacity, you may feel crappy or anxious because you are not pulling in enough oxygen, which allows your emotions to feel out of control. We are not just physical bodies; we are energy beings. Breathing is a manifestation of our vitalizing force, or our vital energy, which Eastern Indians call "prana" and the Chinese call "chi." Energy is around us and in every one of our cells and it operates every function in our minds and bodies. We cannot live without it. After two minutes without oxygen, we start to check out. Energy from our surroundings is called cosmic energy, and the energy coming through our feet from the earth is called Teluric energy. Energy is found in all life forms. Energy is not matter itself but rather is the energy that animates matter. If there is no oxygen flowing in our bodies, there is no life in our bodies. We also get energy from food and water. They are all the mediums through which energy flows to us. That is why pure water, clean air, and foods free of harmful chemicals are so important. They support our very cells. Everything works together as a whole, with each manifestation supporting the others. We call this universal energy. It manifests itself as gravitation, electricity, the physical actions of our bodies, our nerves' impulses, and thought force. The control of this vital energy opens the door to unlimited power. Gradually, by breathing appropriately, we can control all our energies and thoughts to raise our levels of consciousness.

People with plenty of this energy, which is stored mainly in the solar plexus, radiate a vitality and strength which can be felt by people and animals around them. Have you ever noticed how some animals are attracted to some people? Or have you met someone you automatically felt you could be friends with? Such attraction is due to life energy. People who radiate in this way are broadcasting their life force, or prana. The highest form of this energy is thought, and the lowest is breathing. The control of these vital energies can open amazing doors for us. By learning to control our breath, we can learn to control our life forces, such as pain, anxiety, stress, and healing for ourselves or others. Breathing keeps the body alive through energizing the whole system. As we learn different breathing techniques, we empower our prana, or chi. Have you ever seen people who can't breathe well or who can hardly stand straight? When we do not stand tall, our breathing is inhibited because our lungs cannot fully inflate. Standing up straight helps our breathing and allows our breath to reach all of our cells. Smoking may not bother us while we are young because our bodies are more resilient then. But as we get older and we cut more and more oxygen out of our systems, we become weaker and less able to direct our energies where they need to go in order for us to function properly, decreasing our life force—which is the other name for prana, or chi.

UFOs

Q. Do you believe in UFOs?

A. If you mean UFO's as in Little Green Men, there is always a possibility! Look at the stars on a clear night and see billions of them sparkling. We can't even count them Do you really think that we are the only planet in all the universes that have living human beings on them or living life somewhere? That's an egotistical bit of thinking. No, it is not sensible to assume we are it! We have always believed that we have a very sensible Creator. It would be a waste of space, time, and energy to not have populated other planets with some kind of living being with some kind of consciousness. Our solar system has been around for many billions of years—more than we can truly calculate. You think nothing had the opportunity to grow and prosper? That is not sensible. We are not the only ones.

I have never seen a UFO that I have any proof of. I have seen strange things in the sky; that's the closest I can get. One time when my kids were small and we were living in the country, the kids were in bed and I went out in the yard after dark, and over the tops of the trees across the road was a strange triangular thing that had three bright lights on its underside. It was slowly moving back and forth quite high over the tops of the trees across the road. I don't know what it was; I had never seen anything like it. I couldn't tell how far away it was. It appeared to be almost overhead. Just for the heck of it, I grabbed my flashlight and started to flash "SOS, SOS, SOS" in Morse code, just for the fun of it to see what would happen. It was the only Morse code I could still remember (although sometimes I get it backward). Suddenly, this triangular thing flew directly overhead and flooded the yard with lights as bright as day and lit up the entire yard and the trees behind the house! It scared the living bejeebers out of me! I'm not sure what it was—our aircraft or something from "away." It left almost instantly. There was no noise and no trail ... just *boop* ... Gone! It never made a noise! I just jumped, and it was gone! At other times I have seen strange things in the sky, but I have no idea what they were.

Ed saw many things over the years, and he personally knew some who reported that they had been taken and brought back. I do not have permission to use their names. I have a dear friend who insists he was abducted and brought back as a child, and he seems to have a very clear memory about it. There is no proof, only a very clear memory of what happened. I know him well and believe his memory and how he describes the event. Often people say, "Well, if they're out there, how come we can't see them?" I think this is because they know that at this time in our development as human beings, we would probably try to destroy them. This will be the case until we get to a point where we truly understand what's going on and know they are not going to hurt us. We don't know if they would hurt us, but we assume that if they were going to, they would have by now! That's our assumption anyway. It's not sensible otherwise! There will be a time when we will know. So, in the meantime, I would say don't worry about it. Because until we get our human race into a place where we are not going to kill everything that moves, we will just never know. It's up to us to get our act together. While we are waiting for 'em to drop in for a cold one, it might be better to practice our welcome speech!

Fear

Q. I have always been told that fear will stop you, or that somehow if you are fearful you can't live to your full potential. I'm scared to death of COVID-19, of losing everything, and of all the hatefulness that's going on. I fear for my family around the country. What can I do to get out of this?

A. Fear is something we all must learn to deal with. Fear is a stopping agent. When we are in fear, we can't function properly. Everything in our lives gets skewed, fear rattles us, and we can't function. Fear is an emotion that may or may not be based in reality. But either way, it will stop our wholesome energy flow. When Jesus told Peter to come across the water from his boat, he did (Matthew 14:22–33). His Lord told him to come, and of course he did; then he realized he was walking on water. He freaked out and started to sink. Jesus told him not to fear, but to come to him. Peter continued to walk to Jesus as soon as he trusted and let go of fear. Fear is a mind thing. We can choose whether to be fearful or not. Our minds do not know the difference between what is real and what is not real. If we experience a situation that hurts us emotionally or physically—a relationship or accident, for example—our bodies will heal. But whenever we think of the situation in our minds, it will feel just as real as the original happening. Continually talking about how bad a situation is, is called "awfullizing." We all tend to do it, especially when we feel supported in talking about negative events. By constantly pushing the negative narrative, we keep the cycle going. That's what PTSD is—the mind playing old tapes. We have learned through our work that healing systems like tapping (EFT) and muscle testing (kinesiology) help release us from this never-ending cycle. If we have anxiety around money and things are tight, our bodies respond as if we have *none* or could end up having *none*, and that throws us out of whack. Fear starts running around in our minds, and then we can feel it in our bodies. Our full systems react to everything we think. But if we can find a way to change our emotion to trust, joy, love, or any other positive emotion, our whole systems will change and be uplifted, letting go of fear. If we fall out of a tree as a kid, we may end up with a fear of heights even though we do not remember the tree incident or see the connection between the incident and the fear. But working with various holistic treatments can remove that core fear, and the fear of heights—the fear of falling—can be healed.

When I get into that fearful space, which we all do, I go to a quiet place—outside, the bathroom, my bedroom alone, or my massage room—and breathe. I do four-square breathing. Breathe out slowly to a count of four, breathe in slowly to a count of four, and repeat four or five times. I put soothing and relaxing music on and think back to a spot of joy in my life. The time of joy could be anything: blowing bubbles with auntie when I was five, getting unexpected flowers for my birthday, or a simple, unexpected compliment that touched me. It only has to be a little thing. It's about the spot of joy or happiness we felt at the time. The positive emotion carries the change. We will feel our self-calm and feel at peace. Our fear will be diminished. We can do this anytime, wherever we are. We may have to change the situation; perhaps we can't lie down with music playing, for example, but perhaps we can sit in our cars and breathe and think positive, loving thoughts about something we care about, such as how very much we love our sweeties, our dogs, or our children. This shifts our energy and lifts our stress sensation. If we make a practice of this simple action, we will get the hang of it. As we let our breath go, our attitudes change, our fear goes, and our bodies get back to running normally, because now, without stress in this moment, there are no blockages, and everything runs smoothly. Until next time.

As we work on this, there will be fewer and fewer next times. So self-talk, positive breathing and changing thought patterns are the path to remember the next time we are frustrated and down.

Sometimes it's good to take even five minutes a day and do this practice, even if we think we don't need it. It will help us all day through. Remember: we are all in this together here on Earth. Currently things are changing rapidly. It feels like a very scary time. Part of what we are learning now is how to recalculate our lives and bring out the compassion and caring that were given us and are in our nature. As I have said before, we all have feelings from which we can learn to feel how others feel, and these feelings can eventually guide us to become a real, loving, and whole Earth community. Since we feel pain and fear, we can learn how not to cause these things in others as well as how to be uplifting to others.

Some years ago, I did a fire walk. There were about forty people involved. We built a huge bonfire. When the coals were at the proper stage, we took turns walking across the fire. I knew it was going to happen. I had signed up for the experience. I worked on my terror all week, talking myself into having courage and being able to follow through. When the time came, I was a wreck! I stood there searching for the courage to lift one foot, the heat from the coals burning my face and causing my shorts to stick to my sweaty skin because of the high heat. Looking down to the end of the long path of the bed of coals, I stepped up. I don't remember the temperature—not that it matters, I guess. I was shaking! I put one foot on the coals (*Sh——! I didn't burn!*) and then the other. I was in shock. I didn't burn, and I didn't hurt. I walked the full length! It was so hot that the shirt I was wearing started to smoke on the edges. I walked slowly, placing one foot securely in front of the other. (One should not run when walking on coals; falling would not be good. One's clothing could catch fire, and one could be badly injured. So, I did no running, no matter how scared sh——less I was!) As I walked deliberately, I discovered something no one had ever talked about. The coals have a voice! They talk; they have a sound! With each step, it sounded like I was walking on smashed Styrofoam cups! It never occurred to me that hot coals had a sound of their own.

I made it! I did it! I jumped up and down with excitement, and the crew cheered that I had made it through. The next person in line was ready.

What I learned about firewalking and fear is that it is not about control; it's about letting go and trust! The week before, I had been fighting with myself about how to be tough enough to be in control and deal with this. It turned out that letting go of fear and control was the key. Part of our fear exists because we try to control everything. All of us here will die. Period. That's the

141

plan. We have also been taught that we are never good enough to get to the place of glory with our creator, so the expectation is that we must have somehow screwed up along the way. So instead of death being a happy homecoming and a time for acceleration, our passing is shrouded in quaking fear, even for those who feel they did everything right. There is always that question. Our aboriginal peoples took dying as part of life, and when their time came, they left. What came after was accepted as walking on a higher path with the Creator. We have other places to go and other lessons to learn, and besides, we need a break from earthly life. Take a vacation and come back around next time … maybe? We all live as if this is it—do or die! But this is only a tiny part of what there is! Yes, we will leave here, but our lives are not only about being here We have so much to learn and put in practice. Once we are done with this school, we may have an opportunity to apply what we have learned and then come back to learn more, perhaps. Since we are here for a reason, the more we can let go and let fear go, the better and more filled our lives will be, and the more we will understand that much of the extraneous stuff in our lives may not really be important. What is important is relationships. All of us who have lost a loved one know this. So, when I come to a bump in life, I ask myself, "How important is this? Will it make a difference next week, next month, next year, in five years, in ten?" I then make attitude adjustments about the situation in my head. I so hope this helps provide a different insight. Of course, even though I can walk on fire, I constantly burn myself when I use my oven! Go figure! Some things I will never figure out!

More of Our Insight

Even though many of these esoteric teachings are available for those who have the inclination and correct attitude about them, they have been hidden so that only people with pure intent will be trained to use them. As a human race, we are not ready to have this kind of knowledge yet. We still have a way to go at this point before the human race can focus on the peace, love, and enlightenment that this information will bring us. It will be available to everyone; that indeed is the plan. At this point, many are starting to see light, but we are not ready for the whole enchilada! We are not ready to learn en- masse. Some of us are ready to have this kind of knowledge, but not all of us.

If you want to study and learn, there are places to learn and real teachers to teach. We would advise you to be mindful and use common sense in your search. Pay attention to your Innate. Your Innate will tell you whether you are as willful and as cocky as I was in the beginning. It can be shocking when you think you know it all and realize you really don't know much! Your Innate will help you find who is the right teacher for you, and not a charlatan. You will have to study and be very serious to learn everyday practices and understand how you get information and what the basic information is. The things that we've described are answers to your questions, and they're all based in quantum physics (as our limited understanding permits). The ancients didn't use this term, but they had the idea and knew everything was connected. They did not know the word "quantum," and they did not have a concept of tiny invisible dots of energy moving at light speed running everything in the universe. To them it was spirits or the life force of the plants or animals and the spirit of God, or the Creator. They understood that there was nothing but connections to everything by everything. They understood the process and how to work with the connectedness of everything. They were very careful not to teach people that were inappropriate to receive this information. They understood that thoughts, emotions, and feelings were the driving forces that connected everything, love being the greatest of them all. They wanted to make sure that people who wanted to learn for their own good only were not trained in this sacred work. It was kept secret for so many centuries because they knew the value and the strength that absolute gratefulness, love, and compassion would bring about in the world when people had good intentions. If not, it would open the door to disaster. Our time to learn and act is here. We can create peace on Earth one molecule, one photon, one atom, or one cell at a time. With a mass working together, it won't take long to help bring forth the world that was promised to us. But we must do our part to work with the creative forces even though we don't fully understand them yet. We won't understand until we are in a place of true understanding.

As I've been writing this, I have been working on some assumptions. They made sense to us, so I'm offering them as food for thought. We believe that many "teachers" have come to Earth to share and teach us better ways. In our culture, the dominant religion is Christianity. There are many others. The majority in the world believe in one God, and most believe in one Son who came here to teach. But we know there were many teachers sent. We are told that we need to have Christlike consciousness. But what does that mean? Christ was a teacher, a compassionate man, who supposedly preformed miracles. I use "supposedly" here because there is no such thing as a miracle. A miracle is something that happens that we can't explain. Nothing happens outside of natural law. God is natural law. The work the Master did was considered a miracle because nonalive at the time could understand it. But *he* did! Things are set up by our Creator for interaction with the law as we grow to understand what that is. From what we have gathered over the years, and with our limited understanding of quantum science, I would say that the Master was following and using natural law, as did Buddha, Krishna, Moses, the Prophet Muhammad, and many other teachers over the centuries. Our culture mostly accepts Jesus. But there have been others who have come to teach and heal.

Jesus understood the process of combining the knowledge of thought, intention, and concentration. Communicating with his Innate, with the emotion of love behind everything, he created the healings and the "miracles" we saw and learned about. His turning of water into wine was done through a change in chemical molecules. How did he do that? The episode of the fishes and the loaves was an instance of a changing of molecules or assisting the crowd to feel and believe they had been fed by concentrated thoughts. I wasn't there, so I don't know. But based on what little I understand of the quantum world, I believe this is possible.

We all use little bits of this energy when we ask in prayer, when we lay on hands, and when we have a hunch or insight about something, and we can follow through to the expected conclusion. Those are steps. We are learning. When we reach out in even a simple way, with a smile and a thank-you, it makes a difference in the matrix. We know this is true, but we have not yet learned its full force and impact. It is at our very fingertips. We think this is what is meant by Christlike consciousness. He could do these things to give us a clue as to which way to go and what to strive for. He offered us a way to understand the truth about our lives and all creation through the universe, even with our limited human thinking. He also did these things to prove they could be done. He said, "As I do you can do as well" (Matthew 7:12, paraphrased).

I think we, as a race, are on this path. God is not going to hurt us or punish us if we don't get it for a while. God is not a person. God does not have human emotions and will not get mad with us and punish us like an angry parent, even though that is what most of us have been taught. Humans have made a God of love into a scolding, angry parent with all the dysfunctionality of a human parent. God, or the Creator, is pure love energy. Laws and rules have been put in place. We have free will to either learn and

145

practice or not. As we learn to tap into this unbelievable matrix, we will learn how to live and spread only love. (We still have a way to go!) We are part of the whole system. We believe that God is the total energy of everything. It is consciousness itself. That is the force that drives us and heals us. We are part of the God creative force, still using baby steps. Many of us have learned that God is always within. Since God created us in his image, do we have his DNA within us? Some say yes. This makes sense to me. The truth is in our DNA and will be found. Some already have an inkling of this to come. When we study our scriptures, we can look at the parables and metaphors that were placed there to bring about knowledge of our truth as we come to understand them over time as more knowledge opens our eyes. These contain so many ideas and theories. There is so much to learn and study. It is so amazing. This is something that we can connect with in our thinking. We will continue to move forward.

Amazing Phenomena

Meeting Maggie

Ed

After Great-Great-Grandmother passed, we moved into a very large fourteen-room house near the water in Harrington, Maine. It was the most beautiful house we had ever had. It had a cupola and a widow's walk. I guess I was a bit precocious as a child, but I knew the cupola would be mine. I was soon to find out I had a roommate. I was okay with that. It was here that I met Maggie. Maggie had lived there in the 1890s, in this amazing 1800s ship's captain's home. She inhabited the widow's walk at the very top of the house. That also turned out to be my bedroom. Soon after I had moved into "the walk," she presented herself to me. She seemed to be cloaked in light. When I finished with all the usual stuff one would do—wiping the eyes, looking away quickly, and then looking back—she introduced herself as Maggie. It seems she and her seafaring husband were the original owners of the property. When he had been at sea for some time, she would come upstairs to her little spot and sit with a spyglass in hand, scanning the horizon for her husband's ship. In those days of sailing ships, Ship Captains homes had a large cupola with windows on the roof of the house, where the wife would look for the flag of her husband's ship coming in. There was no communication in those days. If the ship did not arrive when due, it would be assumed he went down at sea. When it would come to be overdue for more than a few days, she would start pacing back and forth. As her sisters before her and after would do, she walked.

One night we met on the narrow stairs leading up to the room. I was excited by this encounter. We talked about many different things. I went to my folks and told them about it. Being good fundamentalist Christians, they were horrified. I was punished with soap in my mouth as if I had said a bad word or something. They told me that I would never speak of such things again. They told me there were no such things as ghosts and that it was only a demon trying to get me.

Two nights later, the house was awakened by a terrifying scream. It was coming from the rooms of a missionary boarder that was staying with us for the summer. Mom opened the door, and the young lady was on her knees in the middle of the bed, screaming as the head of the bed rose into the air and came down with a thud! It did that a couple of more times before Dad could get her off the bed and out of the room. As I was climbing the stairs back to bed, not that I would get any sleep anyway, Maggie and I met. We laughed till I almost peed my pants. We sat up and talked the rest of the night—a ten-year-old boy and a one-hundred-year-old ghost chatting about all manner of things. The missionary girl took what she could grab and went back to NYC nonstop from northeast Maine, never to show her face again. I don't know what stories she told the people at church school, but I bet they were doozies!

Did Someone Say Orange?

Sonja

I was working in my office in an old warehouse, focusing on getting a bunch of paperwork done. Suddenly I smelled the delicious aroma of fresh orange. I stepped out of my office and asked people in the adjoining offices and cubicles whether anyone was eating an orange for lunch. No one on that floor was. Seeing as the building was an old, remodeled warehouse, the structure was fairly porous. So, a couple of us went downstairs, being silly, and asked all the people there whether they were eating that tasty orange we could all smell for lunch—you know, just in case they wanted to share. Nope. No one had anything resembling an orange. But we could all smell it, even on that floor. It was like an orange bomb had gone off, filling the entire building. We looked for room freshener, incense, orange floor cleaner, or furniture polish, as well as any other thing we could think of that would make that freshly peeled orange smell. No luck. We all went back to work still smelling that delicious aroma.

As soon as I settled in and focused on my work schedule, my phone rang. The voice on the other end said, "How did you like your orange?" I could hear the ear-to-ear grin in Fuzz's voice. My normally persistent voice was silenced. I was in shock. He said again, "Well, how did you like your orange?" When I could finely speak, I told him what had happened. He then started to explain that he had gone into a meditation holding an orange in his hand and had visualized the scent filling the room I was in. He knew fresh orange was one of my favorite scents. It reminded me of love, happiness, and freshness. He did not expect the entire building to be filled; nor did he expect others to have the same experience! I was amazed. So was he.

Years later, when I started to understand the concepts of quantum mechanics, which describes the world of the very small—the submicroscopic world of elementary particles, electrons, atoms, and molecules, as well as the properties of light at the level of single photons—I came to understand that we are all amazingly connected. We are all truly connected, and when a person affects one proton, even with one's thoughts, other protons are also affected. This was proven scientifically at CERN in Switzerland in 1992. Physicists were doing an experiment with photons, and they shot one through a double slit to see which way it would go. Amazingly, it changed its behavior when it was being observed. Just because someone was looking at it, it changed its behavior! There are bits of energy that we humans cannot see with our eyes; we need powerful microscopes to see these tiny beasties. Yet this photon seemed to know it was being watched, and it changed its behavior! This is a simple description of something very serious, but it's the best description I can offer, not being a physicist myself. Think of what this could mean. Think about how we all affect each other on a subatomic level.

We never think about the tiny physical parts of our lives and how we respond to the effects of others, on an energetic or spiritual level. Nor do we really "get" how we affect others, even with our minds, through what we think, say, and feel. It is amazing if you try to puzzle it out. Most of us can't. So, who or what created these things that make a profound difference to all of us, even though they are nothing we can see and we cannot even understand how these invisible bits of energy affect our lives or the parts we play in directing them? What an amazing creator! Just think, the more we understand about life, spirit, and our Creator, the more we get to play in this world and the more peace we can create with our free will and understanding.

Jumping Face!

About two weeks later, there was an incident that I can only call "jumping face." While I was in Maine and Ed was in Florida, I was lying on the futon in my home office, just resting, not doing anything. I was just thinking random thoughts about nothing when suddenly the wall in front of me opened! I saw a giant wave roll up from the bottom of the ocean and splash me! I felt the wave hit as I gasped for breath, and my fuzzy guy's face was right there in the middle of the giant wave! I jumped off the futon as though I had actually been hit. As soon as I caught my breath, I realized there was nothing there. I felt my clothing; I was as dry as a bone. My heart was racing, and I couldn't stop shaking. A few minutes later, my phone rang, as I picked it up, I yelled, "What the hell is going on?" I knew it was him. I was still in shock. He had scared the crap out of me. He said, "Well, I was walking along the beach and thinking of you. I thought I would try to send you some ocean. I know how much you love it."

Again, quantum mechanics was showing how we are connected. Around this time, scientists were proving that by just thinking about or observing a thing one can make a difference in the thing's behavior.

I meditate a few minutes almost every day, but I have never learned how to meditate into the depths the way he did.

A New Door Opens

When I was in my early twenties, I was getting ready for my brother's wedding. As I was getting my hair done, the lady sitting next to me introduced herself and then told me I was a healer and asked why I wasn't using my gifts. Well, her words scared the crap out of me. I had no idea what she was talking about. It had been years since I had used my gift openly; how would she know? She had not a clue who I was. I figured she was a bit touched, even though I politely wrote down her name and phone number. It was my grandfather on my mother's side who was the healer and physician, not me! It took me two years to finally call her.

It turned out that this lady was a well-known Spiritualist medium. I didn't know what that was, but I made an appointment to see her. I was amazed at what she knew about my life and the things she told me that were to come. Now, she did not know my name before I came to see her. She had no way of checking me out. This was years before cell phones and the internet were the norm. She eventually became one of my teachers.

I had grown up with many different religions in our family, and I had been raised as a Catholic, Lutheran, Baptist, Congregationalist, Methodist, Jehovah's Witness, and Nazarene. I was a Nazarene Sunday school teacher at one time. My mother changed religions as fast as some women, in the day, changed their hats for Sunday service. The good thing about all these religious changes was that I learned a different way of thinking about God and saw how many people around the world have different belief systems and that we can all work together even if our belief systems are not the same. Even though God is the same, we may have our own ways of worshiping.

I had never heard of Spiritualism. But suddenly I met people who saw things and knew things out of the blue, like me. I no longer felt alone. For the first time in my life, I felt supported—not crazy or "woo woo"! The most important things I learned from this group were that the door to reformation was never closed here, or hereafter, and that God is within. We are not doomed to burn in hell. We are loved too much for that. Ed was not a fan of any church group. He believed deeply in God but not in organized religion. To him what was taught in churches did not make sense, and no matter what he did, if anyone found out about his unsolicited gifts, he was considered evil.

Through Ed's travels and training with native shamans, he learned he was not bad or crazy. He came to understand that his abilities were gifts and that he had the free will to hone them to help others. He understood the connection we all have if we choose to use it. Our training was different. Different teachers teach the same truths but teaching styles may be different. In the end, we have the same understanding of how things are put together and what our role as humans on the earth is, as the children of our Creator. Everything connects to everything.

Training Opened My Eyes

Ed

I spent years trying to figure out the how and why of "body flying" (which I learned years later was called "astral flight"), seeing ghosts, and so forth. Body flying happened to me often. I would just be floating above the house or flying over the ocean or to another planet! They were fearful adventures, but only because I was told it was evil and I didn't know how to stop it or what was really happening. I was just a little kid. I told myself that I wasn't evil or crazy, although I was told I was. I learned early not to talk about it to any one at all except my honey-blonde friend. She understood. She had the same abilities. They said she was a witch as well. My church told me I was evil, and my father threatened to beat me within an inch of my life—and I knew he would! But these things happened without my asking or looking for things to happen.

Years ago, long after I had left home and had many other adventures—some great, some funny, and some not so good—I became friends with some who would become lifelong teachers. They had a profound effect on my life. Dan—and I can't describe him more than that, to protect his privacy— even after all these years is still an honored and well-known native shaman. I met him on a movie set where I was a cook. He stayed by himself when he was not working, in his tepee by the fire. I went and sat on the ground near his camp each evening for about a week. I didn't say anything. I just sat near and watched, and when he went to bed, I left and went to bed as well. One evening he asked me what I wanted. I told him I wanted to learn. We talked. We became friends—or rather teacher and student. He took me under his wing and took me into his home with his family. I spent nearly five years with him, learning the ways of shamans. I learned about personal medicine, how to offer prayers of thanks for everything, how we are all connected to each other, to every living thing, and to our creator, the Great White Father. The words "Great White" do not refer to a white person but rather to the light that comes from our Creator. Our Creator always comes as a white light. I learned to mediate—to create a quiet space in which to ask for healing for myself and others. I learned prayers and rituals to continue doing this work. I learned that I could leave my body at will and that I was not bad or crazy, and so very much more. I learned how to go deep within to shut off the pain receptors so I would elevate my old pain from numerous accidents caused by myself or others. He took me with him into the superstitions. On the night of my dream journey, he gave me the name of Star Eyes, Shaman of the People. He said my eyes always looked to the stars.

Another friend of mine was a well-known actor who did commercials about the environment at the time. He was also a friend of Dan. He and his wife were two of my best friends and helped to augment Dan's teachings. During my time with them, I learned about stones, crystals, sage and other sacred plants, the reasons and processes of rituals, the effects they have on people's subconscious minds, and the ways they affect all areas of our lives and psyches. I knew them for many years. I was told by them during a healing circle not to go west. But even with what I had learned, did I listen? No! I figured I knew better! Because I didn't listen, I had some not-so-good life-changing experiences at the invitation of the state for about a year. Not a good time was had by all. I chose to stay in solitary for nearly that whole year. The upside to that is that this "accident" granted me the opportunity to meditate a lot and really learn how to inculcate my new learnings, which stayed with me for the rest of my life. Sometimes solitude is just what is needed.

As kids, Sonja and I, always watched the stars and wondered which stars we came from, wondering whether our "real parents" would ever come to get us. Dan was a great believer. Over the years, the great teachers I have spoken with have almost to a person agreed with my basic philosophy that we are indeed descendants of the equivalent of space gypsies—"Those who boldly go where no man has gone before." As Star Trek would announce. Dan was a great believer in otherworldly origins of species. It makes as much sense as anything else that I've been asked to swallow on blind faith.

Visitations

Sonja

Years ago, I had a friend who was in a barbershop quartet. He lost his voice as a result of cancer as a young man. I met him much later in life and learned his story. He married and had a daughter. He daughter had never heard his natural voice. He spoke with an electrolarynx—a device that is held to the throat and can produce a mechanical voice as air passes over the larynx. About six months after he passed, I was sitting in my living room, just rocking in my rocker, looking out the window and letting myself just be relaxed. I was not thinking about anything consciously when suddenly I heard a man's voice! It said, "I can sing again, and the whole gang is here!" I did not see him, and even though I had never heard his real voice, I knew exactly who it was! I was so happy for him that I just sat there and cried for his joy.

When I was a young women, I woke up one night and my Grandfather, Dada, who had passed when I was about 13, was standing by the side of my bed. He was solid, I could smell he aroma of his rich cigar. He said, "Don't worry he is with us, we have him." I had no idea what he was talking about and wondered why I had dreamt about him after all these years. At day light my phone rang. I learned a family member, a child, had been killed in a freak accident, on the other side of the country. I would have no way of knowing. Except for the visit. As soon as the phone rang, before I answered, I knew what the call was about.

The Dark Side

It was difficult as children to navigate our world while understanding that we were different. We saw fairies, we knew things that happened at home while we were at school, and we had dreams that came true or gave us information about things most kids our age would have no idea of. We learned to keep our mouths shut—to be "good," as we were told. We were fearful that we were wrong, and that God would fry us when we died because we did not obey. We were told that over and over. If there was a real God that we spoke to all the time, who we were told was supposed to love us no matter what because he made us and he loved us so much he let his son be killed so we would live, why would he kill our souls and burn us in hell for ever and ever? That did not seem sensible. We believe we have a sensible creator! Look at how organized the universe is! *Everything* is a mathematical equation! There is so much more to understand than we can even conceptualize at this point in our growth! We and our universes are not random. We are intelligent and awesome creations made in the image of God, *on purpose!*

We tried to be so good and tried to listen and understand what the adults were telling us, but it just didn't make sense! Maybe we were really crazy or as evil as they said! They always said we were witches or worse. They said we were doing bad things. When they found out, we were punished. But we didn't start out trying to be bad. Information just came. We only had each other to share this with. It was so exciting when I touched a tree and started to talk to it. Then suddenly I started getting pictures about the tree—a tree that let me know something as soon I put my hand on its trunk! I knew somehow the tree was alive and felt things and could find a way to tell me.

My only friend said he could fly and showed me how to fly with him. Until then I could only fly close to the ground, my toes touching the ground, kind of pushing me forward at ground level. I got to see a lot of close-up bugs that way! It never occurred to me to just think, *Up!* It was so breathtaking and wonderful.

It seemed so mysterious when one of us knew an unsettling letter had come in the day's mail and no one told us 'cause we were kids and didn't need to know the family business, but as soon as we got into the house we would know we were right. What's a kid to do?

Even with all the stress we were under (although we didn't see it as stress), we had no idea then what the word "stress" even was; we just knew we were in trouble all the time. (We did not realize the impact of always being told we were bad as kids until many years later.) I think the very best fun of all was learning that we could leave our bodies and fly together, 'cause nobody knew! They thought we were asleep in our beds! The odd part was that people, mostly family, would come by when they were ill and ask me to put my hands on them because it made them feel better. Now, if it was family, it was fine, but I could not interact in that way with outsiders, even family friends who came over. I never could figure out why it was okay to touch family but not nonfamily. My step-grandmother, Nana, always said that when I put my hands on her head, her migraines went away. I didn't understand what I was doing; I only knew that I asked God to please make the headache go away, and the headache went away.

When I picked up the raccoon that got stuck in our cellar, I just went over picked him up and put him outside. Everyone had fits, screaming at me that I would get bitten and die. I wasn't scared; I didn't even think about it hurting me. I never thought about rabies. We lived in the country and lived around wild animals all the time. So, I just picked him up in my arms like I would hold the cat. He didn't bite or act as if he were afraid. As soon as I put him down outside, he ran off back into the woods.

After we grew up, we continued to explore other worlds as much as we could. We both over the years, even when we were apart for decades, found ways to study many world religions, cultures, branches of science, and paranormal activities. Some of these things were true; some were tales. But we both searched as far as our unscientific searching would take us. Sometimes our searching was correct, and sometimes it was far-fetched, but we kept trying to figure it out. There were none to talk to us or teach us yet, so we went about our own way of searching and trying to figure things out.

Ed left home when he was sixteen. He traveled and worked in various parts of the country. He worked as a head cook on a shrimp boat, worked in sales, and did various kinds of other work that took him and his Suzuki cross country and eventually brought him to developing and running his own small business. In his travels, he ran into people who had outlooks on life that were different from the strict church ideas he was raised with. It didn't really fit with him, but it was intriguing. These people also had "foresight" and seemed to understand healing energy, or at least energy, which he was just beginning to understand. They were "magic." They knew how to work spells. There was a lot of ceremony and many different rituals—many of them sexual, but to an unknowing young acolyte, this was exciting on so many levels. He thought finding people like him was amazing! As he studied and learned many of the lessons, it became harder and harder for him to leave. He realized this way of using energy was not right. He realized that this was not him and that he needed to leave. Ed became involved with the woman who was the head of the group. When he realized that her vision was not his and that this was not the kind of group he should be involved with, it became harder and harder for him to leave. He was being brainwashed into believing that their form of dark energy was power. They threatened to kill him if he left. They saw in him the ability for real power, and they didn't want to let him go. He was being groomed for a leadership position. When he had the full realization of what was happening, he left. He went into hiding for years, keeping his own light covered. Never using his abilities, least his energy would be picked up and tracked. He ran form the work to keep himself safe. He worked to understand the truth of what had happened to him. It was years before he reconnected with his own energy. Because of the situation with the group, he walked away from the knowledge and abilities he'd had since he was born. He feared they would find him no matter where he was. He left the "craft," never to return. The group and the situation scared him more than his parents admonitions, his dad's belt, or threats from his family's church group. He was done, and he blocked any feelings, visions, or information he was given to know. He only fully came back to what he knew, after we were reunited.

When we were fourteen, our situations changed through no fault of our own. We had no connection with each other for the next forty-seven years. It wasn't until we were in our fifties that we reconnected and finally were able to sort out all the information we had learned or been separated from. We slowly combined lifelong learnings as we started to put our piecemeal knowledge back together.

I took note of what was happening in my life. I tried not to respond to the visions and "knowings" I was receiving. I learned that, for me, rhythm was a key to leaving my body. Rocking in a chair, drumming, and running back and forth on the same path in the yard while softly talking to myself seemed to create a relaxation response that made it possible for me to be in more than one place at a time. I know I was still running back and forth on the path, as I could see myself; but at the same time, I could see from the roof of the house or the top of the tree and watch myself running and hear the little ditty I was mumbling to myself. Dreams came and went, leaving me the task of figuring out what they meant, if I could. Sometimes I would not understand them for weeks or months. Sometimes I would forget about them, and six months later something would happen, and I would say, "Oh, that's what that meant!"

Over time I learned to not pay attention to information I was receiving in dreams or just seemingly random insights during the day. I was mindful that this was often information I needed, but I mostly just let it fly by. I was rattled thinking what if I'm wrong and I'm really going to fry!

As I grew up, it became easier to squash down the visions and feelings. I graduated from nursing school and worked in private duty situations, which gave me a lot of flexibility to care for my kids. I had the time to start studying with a local American Indian, Bill, who belonged to the Spiritualist Church. Amazingly, these people also saw, heard, and felt spirit and could interpret the meanings of what they saw, heard, and felt! At last, I had found people who were not crazy—or at least were only as crazy as I was!

Bill helped me understand my dreams, why information comes in dreams, and many other things that helped me put two and two together. We discussed how plants talk and how and why we can know or understand what they say if we know how to listen. We discussed what the science was that could move physical objects across a room and so very much more. All of that took belief, concentration, understanding, and calmness, as well as a deliberate setting aside of time to learn and to at least have the basic understanding that the quantum field exists. There is a reason we often hear about monks or other religious people going off to a mountaintop or into a cave for years. They do so to focus on the gifts they have been given far seeing, healing, foresight, and so many other attributes that they could not focus on if they were working and caring for a family. They feel they need a place where they can practice and learn about the use of this powerful energy. They believe they are doing a service to God by using their gifts to help humankind. In our lives today, they are many distractions from these abilities. Much of our world has let go of the practice of wholesome living and loving practices.

I was working as a private nurse in a client's home. My job was to stay the night and take care of whatever the client needed. After I tucked her into bed, I would sit on the sofa and read or write research papers I had been working on. There was no TV. The house was old and still had some of the original furniture from the twenties—really cool stuff. One night I was sitting there reading and I heard music—older music from around the turn of the last century. I looked up in shock to see people dressed in clothing of that time sitting in the living room, chatting! There was music coming from someplace, and I just sat and watched them having conversations and laughing and dancing. I was sitting there dumbfounded. They didn't see me, and I could not get their attention. I was just amazed! I had goosebumps all over my body. Suddenly my patient's bell rang. I had to leave the party, but the partygoers never said a word to me. How rude!

Over the weeks, this kind of thing happened often. Sometimes a woman would walk through the room, and sometimes there was faint music most of the evening, although there was nothing in the house that could play music. One night I was stretched out on the sofa. My client had a bell to ring if she needed me, so now and then I could doze a bit during the night. One night I jumped up before the bell rang. I ran into the room just as she reached for it. She never rang it, yet I heard it! Then, a few weeks later, I was dozing while the house was quiet when suddenly there was a black force like a cloud that came over me. The cloud was trying to cut off my air. I felt as if I were dying as the black was covering me and trying choke me. I couldn't move. Suddenly I remembered to use the light. I hadn't done it for so many years, and I didn't think I could remember how. As I calmed myself, letting go of the fear I felt, I remembered how to use the light! I went into the quiet place the that holds the light energy and told it to work, and it did. I felt my body float through the black, and the other side was filled with bright light like you would never believe! It covered the black clouds, and they disappeared. I was there, still lying on the sofa, shaking like a leaf in a thunderstorm. I had felt as if I were dying. I don't know what the force was but getting rid of it reminded me of the energy and abilities I once had. The situation really scared the crap out of me. It was a long time before I figured it out.

I told my spiritual teacher Bill about what happened. He asked permission to smudge the house, and the homeowners allowed it. He did the smudge ceremony, and I never had another problem as long as I worked there. When I asked him about the blackness, he said that I didn't need to know at this time. He said I wasn't strong enough yet. Years later, I found out that someone from my past had learned some negative mystical things and was using black magic to hurt me.

Energy *is!* We control energy with our minds, Energy has no feelings or understanding. Energy takes its direction from us when we ask it to, depending on our intention. That's how prayer works. We become quiet and introspective, and we ask to have a need met. We offer thanks. We pray or ask in the way in which we were taught. We ask for the highest good to be done. Prayer works, as thousands will attest to. But what about when it doesn't? I believe this happens because there is a different path that the situation is meant to follow, and we are not aware of what the highest good is for that situation. Prayer, answered in a way we want it to be answered in or not, still holds to our heart as love given, and it does make a difference even if we don't understand how. Energy does not know good or bad; energy *is*, and it will do what we ask if we understand how to ask. When we ask, our request should come from the emotion we feel in our heart and soul. It's our emotion that gives our thoughts and feelings, power or movement to reach our intended Source. The feeling we project should be one of thankfulness, and gratefulness. Not of fear or lack.

That is one of the reasons people are leery of anyone who may have these true gifts. Most believe that if you can use these abilities for good, you can also use them for bad. Therefore, all people with these gifts could do bad, because they know how. So, the general thinking is that all people who have these gifts will use them as a destructive force. Our Greatest Master always used his gifts for good. We can learn to use them in this way as well. He said, "What I do you can do also, and more" (John 14:12, paraphrased).

At the end of my training with Bill, during our closing ceremony, he blessed me with the name "Star Shine." He said this was because my eyes shone like stars. More than twenty years later, I learned the story of Star Eyes. We were, unknown to each other, given our names at about the same time.

We all have the ability of using our energy or consciousness of free will to help ourselves and others. We have the power to do good, helpful, healing work. Through these gifts, we can help other people and animals, as well as the earth. As I and many others have said, energy can be used as a destructive force as well. Our job is to learn and promote the use of good energy. We do this through our thoughts and intentions. We have been given many gifts; learning to use our God-given energy for the good of ourselves, others, and the earth is part of our learning while we are here. Energy *is*. It is our universe and who we are. Everything has and is energy. Everything vibrates. All energy can be controlled by thought. Thought and consciousness are energy. God is energy. We are energy; therefore, we are part of God or the Creator, creation, and God energy.

More of Our Insight

Right now, the world feels as if its falling apart. It's not. It is being disrupted by lessons that teach us it's time to follow a different path. These are our lessons. No one is doing anything to us. People ask, "Why is God doing this?" What is happening is due to us not using our free will correctly. God is not punishing us. Most of us are choosing to not connect with the energy, because most of the lessons we are here to learn have been changed by others, and some have been hidden. Many of us have lost our connection to our Creator within. We have never totally learned to follow our healing paths. We have the choice to change how we think. All people will have a hard time during the next dozen years or so. Everyone says he or she wants peace on Earth. But few are willing to create it. We have this ability as children of the one God, and we have the right. It is the children coming in now who will be different. They will see the needs and understand how to change our current system at all levels. It will even be found that their DNA is different from ours.

They will see and know what they *don't* want and will take steps to see that those things (e.g., war, crime, hunger, greed, and hurt) are eliminated. But first peace must come from within. Finding peace within comes before finding peace in our world. The new ones will find ways to eliminate fear and all negative things. They will learn that the truth is in their hearts, because we will have taught them to think outside the box and that everything is connected. All life on our planet and our solar system is connected. Our cells, energy, plants, animals, other humans, photons, thoughts, and consciousness are all connected to each other and our whole Earth and universe.

The "new ones" will be released from old dogma. They will learn how to go within to bring peace to themselves so they can teach the older ones how. Once there is peace within, there will be peace without. It is important that those who have the capacity to learn a new way of being and thinking apply it to themselves first. We can all learn as much as we can so we can be teachers of the ones who will make the change and learn how to eliminate fear, want, anger, lack, inappropriate behavior, and incompetent governments. I won't be alive to see these prophecy changes, but you will. You and those like you are part of the new system that will be taught to those coming up. They will be taught to make decisions and actions based on compassion, love, caring, and joy directed to others as well as themselves. The new world and peace and love have been prophesied. Many believe the earth will be destroyed. Earth belongs to God. "He" will not destroy the earth, even though humans are making a mess of it. As humanity moves forward, we will be given the tools to understand how to work together. We already have them. We just don't use them or truly understand them yet. It's a matter of turning on the light switch so we can see what is right in front of our noses. The light starts with us. If we ask, "He" is always there. I will stop talking now.

Passing Thoughts

Ed

I was thinking this morning of our cycle of time and the strangeness of how it has all come about, from small children, knowing what others had no clue of; to students of things that others had no clue of; to students of things that frightened most people of little understanding; to teachers and guides in things so old that many have forgotten their existence. As I considered these things, I encountered some that were analogous of others that have brought forth these things and found within each story a thread of sameness, and the words of one came to the fore: "Suffer The Little children ..." (Matthew19:14)

The wonder of that thought came as a spark of understanding that I have never considered before. The fact, now obvious to me, is that those who would be teachers and sages and guides are "chosen" as children, and the single most deciding factor is the openness of their minds and their ability to imagine things unseen by the masses! Am I late to this revelation, or are there bits here that are truly different thoughts?

I have also come to the conclusion that we waste a lot of time just trying to put things in *our* order. We convince ourselves that life will be better after we get married, have a baby, and then have another. Then we are frustrated that the kids aren't old enough and convince ourselves we'll be more content when they are. After that, we're frustrated that we have teenagers to deal with. We will certainly be happy when they are out of this stage. We tell ourselves that our lives will be complete when our spouses get their acts together, when we get nicer cars, when we are able to go on nice vacations, and when we retire.

The truth is, there is no better time to be happy than right now. If not now, when? Our lives will always be filled with challenges. It's best to admit this to ourselves and decide to be happy anyway, no matter what. One of my favorite quotes comes from Alfred D. Souza. He said, "For a long time it had seemed to me that life was about to begin- real life! But there was always some obstacle in the way, something to be gotten through first. Some unfinished business, time still to be served, or a debt to be paid. THEN life would begin. At last, it dawned on me that these obstacles were my 'life'." This perspective has helped me to see that there is no *way to* happiness. Happiness *is* the way. So treasure every moment that you have, and treasure it more because you shared it with someone special enough to spend your time with. And remember that time waits for no one. So stop waiting until you finish school, until you go back to school, until you lose ten pounds, until you gain ten pounds, until you have kids, until the kids leave the house, until you start work, until you retire, until you get a pet, until you get married, until you get divorced, until Friday night, until Sunday morning, until you get a new car, until you get a new home, until you sell the home you have, until spring, until summer, until fall, until you're off welfare, until the first or the third, until you've had a drink, until you have sobered up, until you die, or until you're born again to decide that there is no better time than *right now to be happy!* Happiness is a journey, not a destination.

Remembering Lessons

Ed

Over the past few days, I have received several "visits" from Iron Eyes, one of my old teachers, all leading up to today. When I came home, I turned on the TV, and there on the screen, in a role I hadn't ever seen him in, he was giving a lesson to a young initiate, reminding me of a time so many years ago ... reminding me of words spoken to me so long ago.

"When the larva turns into a chrysalis, it sheds one skin, and becomes another ... When a chrysalis becomes a butterfly, it sheds one skin and becomes another ... Why do you wish me to retain this skin? When it is my time, I too will shed this skin, and become another ... and when it comes my time, I will shed yet that skin and become another. ... If I thought there was nothing beyond this skin, I would fight valiantly to retain this skin. But I know better, and I know the beauty that I will finally become. ... So, cry not at the shedding of this skin, but rejoice in the beauty of my next one!" I cried for an hour at the memory and laughed at myself for not remembering so simple a lesson. His new skin is indeed beautiful, as his spirit always was. The beauty hidden in each of us can show through when we teach, and our eventual glory is glimpsed by those we touch.

Of course, this was simply a reinforcement of a lesson. He knows the work we are doing and that we are dealing with death regularly. I have carried the name Star Eyes since my spirit quest in the holy mountain of the superstitions outside of Phoenix, Arizona, where I was taken by my two shaman teachers. They said I looked to the stars for all my answers; thence I would be known as Star Eyes, Shaman of the People.

Sonja

Unbeknownst to me during the years we were out of contact, Ed was studying his healing path at the same time I was studying and learning from healers of the Spiritualist tradition as well as a native who was also a Spiritualist. We had abilities as children but didn't know how to direct them. Knowing I "did stuff" would frighten the adults. I tried to keep a lid on it but was not always successful. Sometimes something just popped out, such as, "Oh, did you get a letter from Aunt Lucy?" It didn't arrive until the next day. Oops! caught again!

As children together, after the chores of the day had been done and the little ones had been put to bed, we would lay on the lawn and gaze up at the expansive, star-studded New England sky, talking, wandering, planning, visioning, catching fireflies by starlight and trying to send messages to our "*real* parents up in the stars." We eventually learned different views of the spirit world in different ways. We learned how to weave our paths together later in life. It has been an amazing journey. We are grateful for the path we have been guided on during this lifelong journey, as well as for the love, caring, and support we have received from so many, seen and unseen.

Words of Guidance
from Fuzz

As I continued to work on our book *Journey of the Star Children though Time*, I came across a piece Fuzz wrote a few years prior, at a time when the notion that the word was ending was being propagated and scaring everyone to death. The piece contained his thoughts at that time. His plan was to write articles in our newsletter to share some of his learnings from some of his teachers. Life has a way of moving things around in ways we may not always think of. Fuzz left his body on May 17, 2020 and is out adventuring in many new places. He is no longer bound by the restrictions of Earth and gravity. When we leave our bodies, we become multidimensional. (We are already multidimensional, but most of us don't know it because we have never been taught.) But that is a topic for another time. Some of you who know Fuzz have connected with him in his new life. Some of you have received messages from him. I thank you for sharing his words with me. I know they are authentic. The things you have shared with me, no one on Earth could ever know except me. I thought some of you might find a peaceful path through his footsteps and words of wisdom.

Fuzz's Words

As I sat in my living room on New Year's Eve, I reviewed all the gloom and doom from almost every corner. The world is ending. Life will be unlivable without our computers. Catastrophic things will occur throughout the world, et cetera, ad nauseam! I thought back to the teachings of "the People", Natives I studied with for many years, and the reassuringly positive point of view of the old ones: "To live in harmony with Mother Earth is to live a Holy life and ensures one of continued life in better places." We must all adapt to new (old) ways to view our lives and places in them! The tools have been handed down over the millennia, as have the ways to use them. In these writings, we will endeavor to place before you platters of mind food. You will be asked to draw your own conclusions and to relate any thoughts or questions to us, and perhaps we will be able to have discussions during which we all learn new and wondrous things. I would like to start right off with a question and a possible answer, and then follow up with an affirmation. Question: In the language of the healer, shaman, or spiritualist, what is medicine? Answer: Your medicine is your personal interaction with the "energy field." While the more traditional healer may work with drugs to "kill a disease," the drugs do nothing to cure emotional and psychological scars and fears. Healers work within the energy field and help to align the patient's energy, thereby allowing the mind and body to move into closer synchronicity, producing seeming miracles. In fact, the miracle in such cases is that the patient is finally given the keys to his or her own well-being! To work within the energy field, one must be centered and focused. It is important within any faith or practice that we allow ourselves to easily find that center. I do so with words similar to those below each morning as I greet the beauty of each day. It has been thus through all the exceptional years of my life! It is only when I allow other influences to invade my space that my teachings fall away, and I find myself weakened.

Morning Prayer: As I face the west, Father of all spirit keepers, I am here. Hear me speak. My voice is small, but Father of the four winds, please guide my prayers to the Great Father. As I face north, the Great White, I am here. Hear me speak; hear my words. My soul is as pure as snow you bring. Take my prayers so that I might find wisdom. As I face the east, the way of beginnings and youth, I am here. Hear me speak. Hear my words and show me the way so each day I shall know that I walk in harmony. As I face the south, the way of warmth and life, I am here. Hear me speak. Take my thoughts to the Father so that I may know your warm sun shining on my heart. As I turn my face to the heavens, toward my great-grandfather, I am here. Hear me speak. Father, please accept my heart so that I may know myself as your child and feel your presence in all I do.

May the wind find wings and lift you to the face of your great-great-grandfather, and may he bless you with his wisdom.

—Star Eyes, Shaman of the People

Words of Wisdom from Red Crow

Following is a quote from Floyd Red Crow Westerman of the Hopi tribe. We have said throughout that we are energy. Energy *is*. This is another way to say it: We are spirit. Spirit is all around us and is part of us. We see the words "energy" and "spirit" as the same. We are all connected to everything, in all ways. Neither can ever be destroyed; energy, or spirit, only changes form.

> We were told that we would see America come and go. In a sense, America is dying from within, because they forgot the instructions of how to live on earth. It's the Hopi belief, it's our belief, that if you are not spiritually connected to the earth, and understand the spiritual reality of how to live on earth, it's likely that you will not make it.

> Everything is spiritual, everything has a spirit, everything was brought here by the Creator, the One Creator. Some people call him God, some people call him Buddha, some people call him Allah, some people call him other names. We call him Tunkaschila ... Grandfather. We are here on earth only a few winters, then we go back to the spirit world until our times comes again. The spirit world is more real than most of us believe.

> The spirit world is everything. Over 95% of our body is water. In order to stay healthy, you've got to drink good water. ... Water is sacred, the air is sacred.

Our DNA is made out of the same DNA as the tree. The tree breathes what we exhale, we need what the tree exhales. So we have a common destiny with the tree.

We are all from the earth and when the earth, the water, or the atmosphere is corrupted, then it will create its own reaction. The mother is reacting.

In the Hopi prophecy, they say the storms and floods will become greater. To me, it's not a negative thing to know that there will be great changes. It's not negative, it's evolution. When you look at it as evolution, it's time, nothing stays the same. You should learn how to plant something. That is the first connection.

You should treat all things as spirit, realize that we are one family. It's never something like the end. It's like life, there is no end to life.

—Floyd Red Crow Westerman

Closing

Sonja

As we close this book on our amazing lifelong adventure, I would like to also share the following true story with you. I feel that the information that was given was a blessing that I didn't realize at the time. For me personally, it cemented the idea that we are, always were, and always will be. We are all connected to everything, in all ways, always.

★★★

The girth of the stately elder lay on the cold, wet ground absorbing the earth's moisture. Gone was the pale green of his infancy as his arms grew each day to reach the sky, his feet planted deeply into the nurturing soil of his mother. Gone was the dark green of his youth and adulthood as his arms grew even more strongly upward, swaying toward the life-giving sun. As the excitement in his veins grew, he became more attractive each year, enjoying this new life he had been given again. Birds found homes and squirrels scampered, running, jumping, and leaping from branch to branch with no thought.

His fall colors of brown and muted orange gave way as the cold winter ice and storms worked their way into his nooks and crannies, allowing him to sleep blissfully each winter. As he ripened to the blossoming spring of each new year, new adventurous worlds unfolded. Many deer came to graze on his rich dropped fruit. Plentiful wild rabbits hid behind his huge trunk for safety. Our chickens scratched for bits and bugs under his wide, protecting branches, giving nourishment to both tree and chick. Lady Hawk gracefully made wide circles overhead, keeping her sharp eyes peeled to spy the smallest false move below. Dogs peed on his thickening bark ... well, they did! The children climbed and swung on his strong branches. We sat thankfully in his shade, keeping safe from the high summer sun.

His life was full of wonderment, although he had not moved an inch since he was a seedling. But he knew the time for another journey was near. He could feel it. He had started to creak just a little, and then a lot as he swayed in the storms. He knew. Although he did not know what he knew, he had no fear. He just knew the universe would let him continue.

One night, there was a terrible storm like the ones he had always been strong enough to withstand. But this time the lightning struck him in his heart, and he knew it was time. He lay on the ground, absorbing the moisture as he once had as a seedling. He knew there would be another adventure, although he knew not what it would entail.

Soon they came with saws and axes to help him start his new life. It didn't hurt. He could hear them talking about how wonderful it would be to have him in their homes, keeping them warm this winter. It gladdened his multiringed heart to know he would be useful to other living creatures. He would bring warmth and ash to help others thrive. Smoke and particles would travel the world to help others live in their own ways. He was not finished; he had just moved into another adventure. He could feel pieces of is new life start as his little acorns nestled their small bodies into the rain-soaked ground, getting ready for another season in a new life.

We found him lying there, getting ready this morning, after the terrible storm last night.

★★★

When I put my hands on the fallen tree, these are the pictures of its life that came flooding my brain. I cried for two weeks and had no idea why. I realized in retrospect that this was not just about the tree but about the loss of my husband that would happen a year later, almost to the day. I believe the tree was telling me that we are all connected and always will be. Energy *is*. It can never be destroyed. It only changes form, as do we.

My Little Fuzzy Guy went into a coma on March 30, 2020 and passed on May 17. In reality, he actually left on the thirtieth. He was able to pass a message on to me through a friend who did not know our story. I say this because what she told me was amazing, and she had no way of knowing anything about the situation.

He had been in a coma for several weeks. She called and said she had a message from Fuzz. I rolled my eyes. Why would this lady be getting a message? She said, without prompting, as soon as I had that thought, that he said I was too upset to hear him. That was correct. She said to look for a red box with a brown string. I had no idea what she was talking about. Fuzz and I never went into each other's stuff. We both supported personal privacy. So, I started looking in his dresser. Nothing. I looked in boxes he had stored ages ago. Nothing. Then something told me to look in his nightstand. The top drawer held only medical supplies. The second drawer contained books and stuff. In the third drawer was a white piece of paper. I started to shut the drawer, but something stopped me. I picked up the blank piece of paper and under it found a small, heart-shaped red box with brown string around it. I recognized the box immediately. I hadn't seen it in over twenty years! It was a gift I had given him when we first got back together in our fifties. When I was young, I wore my hair in long braids that he always admired. One day my mother got mad at me; I have no idea why now. She grabbed my braids and whacked 'em off, just like that! I put them in this little red box and just saved them for some day in the future, not having a clue what day that would be. Over forty years later, I gave them to him as a token of our love and friendship over the years. He remembered. He had always had a thing for my braids! I never saw the box again. I never asked. It was a gift, and I didn't want to be rude. I never knew he still had it right by his side every night. This friend would not have had a way to know about the gift on her own.

After he passed, I received messages and insights from him regularly. I often channeled him during the writing of our story. He said that if he had known it would be so wonderful, he would have left sooner. His soul was troubled by all of the misinformation that had been given him over the years. He was human, not perfect. He said he was learning lessons and was sorry for the things he didn't really understand. But he looked forward to returning someday and understood that when his turn came, he would have a different view in his next life. The most wonderful thing for me was to know that he was not in pain. My heart hurts that he is gone but is joyful knowing he is not in pain. I love him so very much; I could not stand to think he was still in pain. He assures me that he is pain free and happy and learning amazing things constantly.

We hope our story has opened some doors for you and given you the courage to think and look outside the box. We are all gifted with this astounding universe.

Thank you for taking the time and energy to read this book. We appreciate you.

With love,
Sonja and Ed (Fuzz)
Star Eyes and Star Shine

Products and Services Available through Healing Focus

Clear Vision: Finding Peace in a Troubled World, by Sonja Christiansen, Infinity Publishing, 2003. Easy, one-step-at-a-time meditation.

7 Steps to Health & Wellness, by Sonja Christiansen, AuthorHouse Publishing, 2016. Follow these seven easy steps and experience life—one you have always dreamed of.

Simply Cards, by Sonja Christiansen, self-published, 2021. A step-by-step guide to reading simple playing cards. Available from Healing Focus.

Healing in The Light, CD, by Sonja Christiansen, produced by Kraity Multimedia, 2000. A guided meditation for healing and relaxation. Available from Healing Focus.

Seminars and Workshops

We offer programs that support and value the distinctiveness of front-line caregivers through our Optimal Living program, which is dedicated to our health-care workers at all levels.

We offer stress management and beginner healing classes for groups of any size.

Healing classes cover modalities such as therapeutic touch and Reiki I, II, and III. Often groups wish to use our programs as fundraisers for the general public to attend. Components can be offered as seminars, workshops, or lectures with Q and A.

Our Newest Program
Finding and Trusting Your Inner Guidance
This seminar will bring you closer to a
happy, comfortable, and fearless life.
The program is based on *Journey of the Star Children through Time.*

Love, Light, and Laughter
Purely for your enjoyment and laughter, we offer authentic wild Maine porcupine eggs, complete with incubator! Choice of boy or girl. They will keep someone in your life laughing! These small eggs are found buried deep in caves along the rocky coast of Maine. Each nickel-sized egg is an exact replica of its prickly parents. No babies or eggs have been hurt in any way during harvest. Each hermetically sealed egg pouch comes with complete directions for care and feeding, family history, and Latin name. "Laughter is the Best Medicine" (Norman Cousins)

Contact us by email at infocussonja@yahoo.com, or call 1–918–917–9191; leave a message and we will return your call.

You can also write to us at the following address:
Healing Focus
161177 N. 4334b Rd.
Tuskahoma, OK 74574

To Our Readers

I wrote this poem as I was sitting on the dunes next to the Atlantic Ocean, letting the sound and spray of the hypnotic waves rock me. I was thinking of my dear friend. I had no idea where in the world he was at that time. But the words came as I wished and wished for him. Years later, I found out that at that moment he was on the West Coast, walking along the water's edge on the shore of the Pacific ...
I put this on the last page so you could frame it and hang it as a reminder to seek peace within, if you choose.
May you always have clear vision.
—Sonja and Fuzz

May you have clear vision
to follow your own path,
to share the gifts
you have been given,
to teach as
you have been taught,
to give as you have been given to,
to care as you have been cared for,
to love as you are loved, and
to follow the path
of the compassionate spirit

—Sonja Christiansen

References

Bellamy, Isabel, and Donald Maclean.
Radiant Healing. Joshua Books, 2005

Church, Dawson. *The EFT Manual.* Fulton,
California: Energy Psychology Press, 2018.

K. Langloh Parker, ed. *Wise Women of the Dreamtime*,
InnerTraditions International,1993.

Nelson, Bradley. *The Emotion Code*, St. Martins Essentials,2019

Silver Birch. *Teachings of Silver Birch.* Hannen
Swaffer's Home Circle, 1938.

Yogananda, Paramhansa. *Autobiography
of a Yogi.* Rider & Co., 1969.

Zukav, Gary. *The Dancing Wu Li Masters.*

Braden. Gregg. *The Devine Matrix.*Hay House, 2007

Wilbur, Ken, *Quantum Questions,* New Science Library, 1985

Markides, Kyrriacos, C, Riding *With The Lion In
search of Mystical Christianity*, Penguin Group, 1995

Long, Max, Freedom, *The Secret Science Behind
Miracles,* Huna Research Publications,1948

~~~

Karyon, Karyon Masters, You Tube, 2021

Resources

Johnathan Goldman, Healing Sounds
tuning forks
https://healingsounds.com

James Nelson
Meditation Warriors
meditation support and information
https://meditationwarriors.org

Background

Sonja A. Christiansen, KRMT

Excellent Speaker
Adult Educator
Trained Karuna Reiki Master Teacher
Therapeutic Touch Practitioner and Trainer.
Emotional Freedom Technique Trainer
Massage Therapist, Former AMTA Member
Stress Management Consultant
Developer of the Focused Healing Method of Energy Healing
Ordained Minister, registered in the
States of Oklahoma and Maine
Notary, State of Oklahoma

Professional History

Sonja A. Christiansen, KRMT
1979–present, Director, Healing Focus Center for Holistic Studies
Recipient, US Women in Small Business Administration Advocate
Award 1995
Registered Karuna Reiki Master Teacher
Member of Governor Angus King's Plus #1 Advisory Committee
Member of several governors' task forces
Holistic consultant to the Island of Pico, Azores
Delegate, White House Conference on Small Business
Teacher of stress management and massage as a cultural exchange
for the Women's Business Development Corp. 1995.
Delegate for People to People in the People's Republic of China,
1989
Advisory board member, Mid-State College, Lewiston, Maine
Financial Development Director, United Valley Red Cross,
Lewiston, Maine, 1994–1998
Marketing Coordinator, United Valley Red Cross, Lewiston,
Maine, 1994–1998

Publications

Optimal Living, column, *Clayton Today*, 2005–2020
Meanderings of an Unkempt Mind, self-published, 2003
Clear Vision: Finding Peace in a Troubled World, Infinity Publishing,
2003
The Healing Focus (online newsletter), 2000
Healing in the Light, CD, Klarity Music, 2000
7 Steps to Marketing Your Bodywork Business, workbook, 2001
"Trade Show Savvy," *Developments*, 1997
"Taking Care of Business," *Developments*, 1996

"Stress!" *Maine Law Review,* 1996

"Stress? Who Me?" *Connections,* 1993

Nesting Loon (photographic print) and accompanying article "Enchanted Lake," *Maine Fish & Wildlife,* 1993

"Burnout, The High Cost of Caring," *Maine Scope,* 1990

Massage: The Healing Touch (family massage video), 1987

"Stress Management," the *Maine Law Review,* 1984

Magic Garden & Healing in the Light, audio cassettes, 1982; CD, 2000

Don't Let the 'Gators Get Ya!, 2008

7 Steps to Health & Wellness, AuthorHouse, 2019

Simply Cards, A Guide to Reading Playing Cards, self-published, 2021

In Focus with Sonja & Ed, weekly newsletter on Facebook

~~~~~~~~~~~~

Harvard "Ed" "Fuzz" Webber, RMT

"Shaman of the People" 1946–2020

Entrepreneurial businessman with a creative soul

Joint owner of Clayton Flea, a creative secondhand store

Marketing Manager for Healing Focus, 2002–2020

Meditation and Healing Hands Instructor at Healing Focus

Member of Clayton Lions Club

Writer for In Focus, Optimal Living, and Healing Focus

Marketing manager for several circuses around the country

Concert and marketing manager for several country music stage shows

Creator of several youth-based support programs

Guest lecturer at the University of Maine and other campuses throughout the country on the topics of healing, energy, and personal medicine

Shaman

Healer

Flyer

Printed in Great Britain
by Amazon